Linux Program Development

a guide with exercises

LAB SOLUTIONS

Jerry Cooperstein

```
/*
 * The code herein is: Copyright Jerry Cooperstein, 2009
 *
 * This Copyright is retained for the purpose of protecting free
 * redistribution of source.
 *
 *     URL:    http://www.coopj.com
 *     email:  coop@coopj.com
 *
 * The primary maintainer for this code is Jerry Cooperstein
 * The CONTRIBUTORS file (distributed with this
 * file) lists those known to have contributed to the source.
 *
 * This code is distributed under Version 2 of the GNU General Public
 * License, which you should have received with the source.
 *
 */
```

Contents

Preface

This is a companion volume to *Linux Program Development, a guide with exercises*, by Jerry Cooperstein, pub. 2009. (**http://www.coopj.com**)

While the solutions to the exercises in that volume can be obtained from **http://www.coopj.com/LPD**, occasional requests for printed copies of the solutions are sometimes encountered. (Not everyone prefers reading on the screen, even today.) Rather than increasing the length of the book enormously, I've decided to make the solutions themselves available in book form.

There is no exposition here, only the statement of the exercises and then the actual code and necessary scripts.

Enjoy!

Acknowledgments

First of all I must thank my employer of over 15 years, Axian Inc (**http://www.axian.com**) of Beaverton, Oregon, for giving me permission to use material originally under Axian copyright and which was developed on its dime. In particular, Frank Helle and Steve Bissel have not only been extremely generous in allowing me these rights, but have been true friends and supporters in everything I've done.

In the more than a decade I supervised **Linux** developer classes for Axian (which were most often delivered through **Red Hat**'s training division), I interacted with a large number of instructors who taught from the material I was responsible for. They made many suggestions, fixed errors and in some cases contributed exercises. Colleagues I would like to express a very strong thank you to include Marc Curry, Dominic Duval, Terry Griffin, George Hacker, Tatsuo Kawasaki, Richard Keech, and Bill Kerr.

I would also like to thank Alessandro Rubini for his warm and generous hospitality when not long after I began teaching about device drivers and **Linux**, I showed up at his home with my whole family. I also thank him for introducing me to the kind folks at O'Reilly publishing who gave me the opportunity to help with the review of their **Linux** kernel books, which has expanded my knowledge enormously and introduced me to a number of key personalities.

The biggest acknowledgment I must give is to the students who have contributed to the material by asking questions, exposing weaknesses, requesting new material and furnishing their real life experiences and needs, which has hopefully kept the material from being pedantic and made it more useful. Without them (and the money they paid to sit in classes and be forced to listen to and interact with me) this presentation would not exist.

I must also thank my family for putting up me with through all of this, especially with my frequent travels.

Finally, I would like to acknowledge the late Hans A. Bethe, who taught me to never be frightened of taking on a task just because other people had more experience on it.

Chapter 1

Preliminaries

1.1 Kernel Versions, Linux Distributions and Procedures

We have tried to keep this material as distribution-agnostic as possible. For all but the most specialized distributions this won't present any inconveniences.

The material has been developed primarily on **Red Hat**-based systems, mostly on 64-bit variants with testing also done on 32-bit systems. But it has also been tested on a number of other distributions. Explicitly we have used:

- **Red Hat Enterprise Linux 5.4**
- **Fedora 12**
- **Centos 5.4**
- **Scientific Linux 5.4**
- **Open Suse 11.1**
- **Debian Lenny**

- **Ubuntu 9.10**

- **Gentoo**

You will need a computer installed with a current **Linux** distribution, with the important developer tools (for compiling, etc.) properly deployed.

Where feasible labs will build upon previous lab assignments. The solution set can be retrieved from **http://www.coopj.com/LPD**. As they become available, errata and updated solutions will also be posted on that site.

Lab **solutions** are made available so you can see at least one successful implementation, and have a possible template to begin the next lab exercise if it is a follow up. In addition, **examples** as shown during the exposition are made available as part of the SOLUTIONS package, in the EXAMPLES subdirectory. Once you have obtained the solutions you can unpack it with:

```
tar zxvf LPD*SOLUTIONS*.tar.gz
```

substituting the actual name of the file.

In the main solutions directory, there is a **Makefile** which will recursively compile all subdirectories. By default all sub-directories are recursively compiled, but one can narrow the choice of directories:

```
make SDIRS=s_22
make SDIRS="s_0* s_23"
```

The **genmake** script in the main directory is very useful for automatically generating makefiles, and is worth a perusal.

One should note that we have emphasized clarity and brevity over rigor in the solutions; e.g., we haven't tried to catch every possible error or take into account every possible system configuration option. The code is not bullet-proof; it is meant to be of pedagogical use.

If you have any questions or feedback on this material contact us at *coop@coopj.com*.

Chapter 2

Compilers

2.1   Lab 1: Compiling

- Make a simple **hello world** program. Compile it and execute it. The purpose of this exercise is just to make sure your compilation environment is working.

lab1_hello.c

```
/* Copyright 2009, J Cooperstein coop@coopj.com (GPLv2) */

/* Compile with:  gcc -O2 -Wall -pedantic -o lab1_hello  lab1_hello.c */

#include <stdio.h>
#include <stdlib.h>

int main ()
{
    printf ("hello world\n");
    exit (0);
}
```

2.2   Lab 2: Compiling with headers

- Using the previous hello program as a starting point, put some functions in a separate source file. Also use a header file. Compile and execute it.

lab2_hello_main.c

```
/* Copyright 2009, J Cooperstein coop@coopj.com (GPLv2) */

/*  Compile with: gcc -Wall -pedantic -o hello_main hello_main.c hello_sub.c
 *
 * (If you use #include <hello.h>, you need the -I. option.)
 */

#include "lab2_hello.h"

int main ()
{
    hello_sub ();
    exit (0);
}
```

lab2_hello_sub.c

```
#include "lab2_hello.h"

void hello_sub ()
{
    printf ("\n%s\n\n", hello_string);
}
```

lab2_hello.h

```
#ifndef _HELLO_H
#define _HELLO_H                 /* so we don't get included more than once */

#include <stdio.h>
#include <stdlib.h>

#define hello_string "hello world"

void hello_sub ();

#endif
```

Chapter 3

Libraries

3.1   Lab 1: Libraries

- Use the simple **hello world** program from the previous lesson. Make a static library out of the functions, and compile and link to it.

- Do the same with a shared library.

lab1_hello_main.c

```
/* Copyright 2009, J Cooperstein coop@coopj.com (GPLv2) */

/*  Compile with: gcc -Wall -pedantic -o hello_main hello_main.c hello_sub.c
 *
 * (If you use #include <hello.h>, you need the -I. option.)
 */

#include "lab1_hello.h"

int main ()
{
```

```
    hello_sub ();
    exit (0);
}
```

lab1_hello_sub.c

```
#include "lab1_hello.h"

void hello_sub ()
{
    printf ("\n%s\n\n", hello_string);
}
```

lab1_hello.h

```
#ifndef _HELLO_H
#define _HELLO_H                    /* so we don't get included more than once */

#include <stdio.h>
#include <stdlib.h>

#define hello_string "hello world"

void hello_sub ();

#endif
```

3.2   Lab 2: Dynamical Loading

- Make a simple shared library (libhello_dl.so) that has a "hello world" print function, and one or more constructor and destructor routines.

- Make a test program that dynamically loads the library and executes the function in it.

lab2_dll_lib.c

```
 /* Copyright 2009, J Cooperstein coop@coopj.com (GPLv2) */

#include <stdio.h>
void hello_dl ()
{
    printf ("\n%s\n\n", "hello world from a dynamic library\n");
}

void my_init1 (void) __attribute__ ((constructor));
void my_init2 (void) __attribute__ ((constructor));
void my_init1 (void)
{
    fprintf (stderr, "I entered the first constructor function \n");
}
void my_init2 (void)
```

```
{
    fprintf (stderr, "I entered the second constructor function \n");
}

void my_exit1 (void) __attribute__ ((destructor));
void my_exit2 (void) __attribute__ ((destructor));
void my_exit1 (void)
{
    fprintf (stderr, "I entered the first destructor function \n");
}
void my_exit2 (void)
{
    fprintf (stderr, "I entered the second destructor function \n");
}
```

lab2_dll_main.c

```
/* Copyright 2009, J Cooperstein coop@coopj.com (GPLv2) */

#include <stdio.h>
#include <stdlib.h>
#include <unistd.h>
#include <dlfcn.h>

#define LIBNAME "./libhello_dl.so"

int main (int argc, char *argv[])
{
    char *err;
    void *handle;
    void (*printit) (void);

    handle = dlopen (LIBNAME, RTLD_LAZY);
    err = dlerror ();

    if (err) {
        fprintf (stderr, "error opening library is  %s\n", err);
        exit (-1);
    }

    printit = dlsym (handle, "hello_dl");

    err = dlerror ();
    if (err) {
        fprintf (stderr, "error getting symbol is  %s\n", err);
        exit (-1);
    }

    printit ();

    dlclose (handle);

    exit (0);
}
```

Chapter 4

Make

4.1   Lab 1: Make (Simple)

- Construct a Makefile for the previous section's exercise. It should have several targets, including the application built using either a static or shared library.

lab1/Makefile

```
CFLAGS= -O2 -Wall -pedantic -I.

# static library:

all: lab1_static lab1_shared

lab1_sub.o:  lab1.h

liblab1_static.a:        lab1_sub.o
        ar rv liblab1_static.a lab1_sub.o

lab1_static:        liblab1_static.a lab1_main.c
        $(CC) $(CFLAGS) -o lab1_static lab1_main.c \
```

```
        -L. -llab1_static


liblab1_shared.so.1.0:  lab1_sub.c lab1.h
        $(CC) $(CFLAGS) -fPIC -I. -shared -Wl,-soname,liblab1_shared.so.1 \
           -o liblab1_shared.so.1.0  lab1_sub.c
        rm -f liblab1_shared.so liblab1_shared.so.1
        ln -s liblab1_shared.so.1.0 liblab1_shared.so
        ln -s liblab1_shared.so.1.0 liblab1_shared.so.1


lab1_shared: liblab1_shared.so.1.0 lab1_main.c
        $(CC) $(CFLAGS) -fPIC -o lab1_shared -I. lab1_main.c \
           -L. -llab1_shared -lc


clean:
        rm -f *.o *.a *.so* lab1_static lab1_shared
```

4.2   Lab 2: Make (Complicated)

- Construct a program that has the following properties:

  - There should be a number of different functions, or source files.
  - They should require the use of a number of header files.
  - The source files should be in more than one directory, say a main directory and one or more subdirectories.
  - There should be at least one library with more than one subprogram in it.

- The exercise (besides writing the code) is to construct the Makefile(s) necessary to accomplish this project. You will then compile and execute it. Along the way you'll gain experience with what happens when you change only one file, how dependencies are set up, etc. Note that because of the built-in Makefile rules, you may not need to specify (if you don't want to) exactly how to compile etc, or make libraries, etc.

lab2/Makefile

```
CFLAGS = -O2 -pedantic -Wall
TARGET = lab_program
LIBDIR = ./lib
LIBS   = -L $(LIBDIR) -llabsub
MYLIB  = $(LIBDIR)/liblabsub.a
SRCS   = lab_progmain.c
HFILES = lab_progmain.h

ALL:        $(TARGET)

$(TARGET):        $(SRCS) $(HFILES)  $(MYLIB)
        $(CC) $(CFLAGS) -o $(TARGET) $(SRCS) $(LIBS)

$(MYLIB):
        $(MAKE) -C $(LIBDIR)
```

```
clean:
        rm -f $(TARGET)
        $(MAKE) -C $(LIBDIR) clean
```

lab2/lib/Makefile

```
ALL: liblabsub.a

sub1.o:         subhead1.h
liblabsub.a:         sub1.o sub2.o
        ar rv liblabsub.a sub1.o sub2.o

clean:
        rm -f *.o *.a
```

Chapter 5

Source Control

5.1   Lab 1: Version Control with Subversion

- First you'll need to create a central repository:

```
$ svnadmin create my_repos
```

putting in whatever path you want for the last argument. Take a look at the directory tree created under there. Note that one should never manually edit the contents of the repository, but really on the tools that are part of the **Subversion** package.

- Now you have to create a **project**, consisting of files and directories which you will import into the **Subversion** repository. For example:

```
$ mkdir my_project
$ cp -a  [whatever files and dirs you want] my_project
```

Note that we are keeping things simple; the recommended route is to create three subdirectories (`branch`, `tags`,`trunk`) and to put your files in the `trunk` subdirectory because this convention is often followed; however, **Subversion** doesn't require it.

- Now it is time to import data into the repository with:

```
$ svn import my_project file:///tmp/SVN/my_repos -m "Original Import"
```

where the last argument just gives an identifying string. This will tell you about all the files it added, and if you examine the repository you can see where things went and what some of the other files created and modified look like.

- Now lets checkout a copy of the project so we can work on it and modify it. Do this with:

```
$ svn checkout file:///tmp/SVN/my_repos/ my_project_work
```

Compare the contents of the working copy with the original project. You'll notice each subdirectory has a .svn subdirectory with revision control information.

- Now make some changes to the contents of the files in the working copy. Execute

```
$ svn diff
```

(in your main source directory) to see the changes. Run

```
$ svn commit -m "I made some changes"
```

to place your changes in the repository. If you want to update your copy to whatever the most recent version is in the repository, you do it with

```
$ svn update
```

- We could do a lot more, but this should get you started.

5.2   Lab 2: Version Control with git

- Your system may already have **git** installed. Doing `which git` should show you if it is already present. If not, while you may obtain the source and compile and install it, it is usually easier to install the appropriate pre-compiled binary packages.

- For **RHEL**-based systems (including **CentOS**) the easiest way is to use the **EPEL** repository. Obtain the **rpm** for installing the repository from **http://fedoraproject.org/wiki/EPEL**. Then `yum install git` will accomplish installation. For **Fedora**-based systems the same command will work and there is no need to use **EPEL**.

  For **Debian**-based systems (including **Ubuntu**) it should be sufficient to do `apt-get install git-core`.

  For **Suse**-based systems, one can do `zypper install git-core`.

- Now we can proceed, First we'll have to make a directory to work in, and then initialize **git**:

```
$ mkdir git-test ; cd git-test
$ git init
```

- Next we have to add some files to our project:

```
$ git update-index --add [whatever files you want]
```

- Now we modify one of the files in the project; perhaps something like:

```
$ echo "An extra line" >> [one of the project files]
```

and see the difference with the original repository created with:

```
$ git diff
```

- To finish setting up the repository we do:

```
$ tree=$(git write-tree)
$ commit=$(echo 'The Initial Commit' | git commit-tree $tree)
$ git update-ref HEAD $commit
```

Doing `git diff HEAD` will also show us the changes now.

- To actually commit the changes to the repository we do:

```
$ git commit
```

If we now do `git diff` we"ll see no changes with the committed repository. To see the history we can do:

```
$ git log
```

and for a detailed history:

```
$ git whatchanged -p
```

Chapter 6

Debugging

6.1   Lab 1: Debugging Memory Overruns

- Consider the following test program, which has a memory overrun error:

```
#include <stdio.h>
#include <stdlib.h>
#include <unistd.h>
#include <malloc.h>

int main (int argc, char *argv[])
{
    char *buf;
    int size = 800, index = 801;
    if (argc > 1)
        index = atoi (argv[1]);
    if (argc > 2)
        size = atoi (argv[2]);
    buf = malloc (size);

    printf ("I allocated  %d bytes, I'm going to use the %d element\n",
```

```
            size, index);
    buf[index] = 1;
    printf ("buf[index] = %d\n", buf[index]);
    exit (0);
}
```

- If run with no arguments it tries to write 1 byte over the edge of an allocated array; if run with arguments you can specify the byte to write to and the size of the array.

- Compile it with the **-g** option, and run it under **gdb** (You'll probably want to use **kdbg** or **ddd** as a graphical front end.)

- You can familiarize yourself with using the debugger, trying basic navigation, like stepping through, using next, introducing breakpoints, examining source, etc.

- If compiled with the standard **malloc()** function, you probably won't get any errors for slight overruns.

- Do the same thing but compile using **ElectricFence** (**-lefence**).

- Now run under **valgrind** and see what information can be obtained.

6.2   Lab 2: Debugging Memory Leaks

- Consider the following application, which introduces memory leaks (in this case, allocated arrays which are never freed once they are no longer needed.)

```
#include <stdio.h>
#include <stdlib.h>
#include <unistd.h>
#include <malloc.h>

void doit (void)
{
    char *buf;
    buf = malloc (1000);
}

int main (int argc, char *argv[])
{
    int j;
    for (j = 0; j < 10; j++) {
        doit ();
        printf ("I allocated the %3d buffer\n", j);
    }
    exit (0);
}
```

- Fire up **valgrind** and trace the memory leaks.

Chapter 7

System Calls

7.1   Lab 1: Using strace.

- **strace** is used to trace system calls and signals. In the simplest case you would do:

  ```
  strace [options] command [arguments]
  ```

- Each system call, its arguments and return value are printed. According to the man page:

- *"Arguments are printed in symbolic form with a passion."*
  and indeed they are. There are a lot of options; read the man page!

- As an example, try

  ```
  strace ls -lRF / 2>&1 | less
  ```

  You need the complicated redirection because **strace** puts its output on `stderr` unless you use the `-o` option to redirect it to a file.

- While this is running (paused under **less**), you can examine more details about the **ls** process, by examining the **/proc** filesystem. Do

```
ps aux | grep ls
```

to find out the process ID associated with the process. Then you can look at the pseudo-files

```
/proc/<pid>/fd/*
```

to see how the file descriptors are mapped to the underlying files (or pipes), etc.

7.2   Lab 2: Using syscall().

- The indirect system call function:

  ```
  #include <unistd.h>
  #include <sys/syscall.h>

  int syscall (int call_number, .... );
  ```

  can be used to invoke any system call known to the system. The first argument `call_number` can be read from the list in **/usr/include/bits/syscall.h**:

  ```
  ....
  #define SYS__sysctl __NR__sysctl
  #define SYS_access __NR_access
  #define SYS_acct __NR_acct
  #define SYS_add_key __NR_add_key
  #define SYS_adjtimex __NR_adjtimex
  #define SYS_afs_syscall __NR_afs_syscall
  #define SYS_alarm __NR_alarm
  #define SYS_brk __NR_brk
  #define SYS_capget __NR_capget
  ....
  ```

  The remaining variable number of arguments (indicated by ....) are the arguments to the actual system call.

- This function is not meant to be widely used; it is there for the use of library writers, so don't use it in normal programs unless absolutely necessary.

- Write a program that invokes `syscall()` to run some common system calls. For example you might do:

  ```
  pid = syscall(_SYS_getpid);
  ```

lab2_syscall.c

```
/* Copyright 2009, J Cooperstein coop@coopj.com (GPLv2) */

#include <stdio.h>
#include <stdlib.h>
#include <unistd.h>
#include <sys/syscall.h>

int main (int argc, char *argv[])
```

```
{
    int rc;
    time_t t;
    unsigned long cwd_size = 1024;
    char cwd[cwd_size];

    rc = syscall (SYS_getpid);
    printf ("rc from getpid= %d\n", rc);

    rc = syscall (SYS_getppid);
    printf ("rc from getppid= %d\n", rc);

    rc = syscall (SYS_time, &t);
    printf ("rc from time= %d\n", rc);
    printf ("t from time= %ld\n", (long)t);

    rc = syscall (SYS_getcwd, &cwd, cwd_size);
    printf ("rc from getcwd= %d\n", rc);
    printf ("getcwd gives = %s\n", cwd);

    exit (EXIT_SUCCESS);
}
```

Chapter 8

Memory Management and Allocation

8.1 Lab 1: Examining malloc() Behaviour

- Write a program that uses `mallinfo()` and/or `malloc_stats()` to examine the system's allocation behaviour.

- Try allocating a small, medium, and large amount of memory and see how much is allocated by resizing the data segment as compared to memory mapping.

- Try using `mallopt()` to either turn off memory mapping altogether or to change the threshold between the two techniques.

lab1_malloc.c

```
/* Copyright 2009, J Cooperstein coop@coopj.com (GPLv2) */

#include <stdio.h>
#include <stdlib.h>
```

```
#include <malloc.h>
#include <unistd.h>

#define PRINTIT(a) fprintf(stderr,"        " #a     "\t= %d", mi->a);

void dump_mi (struct mallinfo *mi)
{
    PRINTIT (arena);
    PRINTIT (ordblks);
    PRINTIT (smblks);
    fprintf (stderr, "\n");
    PRINTIT (hblks);
    PRINTIT (hblkhd);
    PRINTIT (usmblks);
    fprintf (stderr, "\n");
    PRINTIT (fsmblks);
    PRINTIT (uordblks);
    PRINTIT (keepcost);
    fprintf (stderr, "\n");
}

void doit (int bytes)
{
    char *buf;
    struct mallinfo mi;
    fprintf (stderr, "\n Allocating %10d bytes ------- \n", bytes);
    buf = malloc (bytes);
    malloc_stats ();
    mi = mallinfo ();
    dump_mi (&mi);
    free (buf);
}

int main (int argc, char *argv[])
{
    int thresh, rc;
    if (argc > 1) {
        thresh = atoi (argv[1]);
        rc = mallopt (M_MMAP_THRESHOLD, thresh);
        fprintf (stderr, "rc=%d from requesting mmap"
                " for more than thresh=%d bytes\n", rc, thresh);
    }
    doit (13);
    doit (13 * 1024);
    doit (13 * 1024 * 1024);
    exit (0);
}
```

8.2   Lab 2: Running Out of Memory

- Write a short program that allocates memory in chunks until the system can no longer obtain any more.

- Eventually the **OOM** killer should be invoked. Look at /var/log/messages to see what decisions it made about what to processes to exterminate.

- Try this with **swap** turned off and on, which you can do (as root) with swapoff -a and swapon -a.

lab2_oom.c

```
/* Copyright 2009, J Cooperstein coop@coopj.com (GPLv2) */

#include <stdio.h>
#include <stdlib.h>
#define MB (1024*1024)

int main ()
{
    int j;
    char *buf;
    /* allocate 4 MB at a time */
    for (j = 0;; j++) {
        if (j%100 == 0)
            printf ("%d ", j);
        buf = malloc (MB);
    }
    exit (0);
}
```

Chapter 9

Files and Filesystems in Linux

9.1   Lab 1: Using the loopback Filesystem

- The **loopback** filesystem driver can be used to mount a file to be used as a hard disk image. This can be very useful for mounting **CD** or **DVD** images as filesystems as well as for simulating or learning about various types of filesystems.

- First you'll have to create a file to use for the image and it is best to fill it with zeros by doing:

```
# create a 200 MB loopback file

$ dd if=/dev/zero of=/tmp/fsimage bs=1024 count=204800
```

- We can then create an **ext3** filesystem on it with:

```
$ mkfs.ext3 /tmp/fsimage
```

and mount it (as **root**) with:

```
$ mkdir /tmp/mnt
$ mount -o loop /tmp/fsimage /tmp/mnt
```

and one can verify its mounting and check capacity with:

```
$ df /tmp/mnt

Filesystem     Type    1K-blocks        Used Available Use% Mounted on
/tmp/fsimage   ext3       198337        5664    182433   4% /tmp/mnt
```

- You may now go ahead and create files, read and write them etc. Such files will survive unmounting (with **umount /tmp/mnt**) and remounting in any location.

- You can do this with other filesystem types as long as you have both kernel support for them (examine **/proc/filesystems**) and the appropriate tool for formatting, such as **mkfs.ext4** or **mkfs.vfat**, etc.

Chapter 10

File I/O

10.1   Lab 1: Files

- Write a program that opens an existing file for read-only and displays it in hex.

- Use the **Unix** API (not ANSI C) for file I/O.

- You can check your results with **hexdump**, but be careful about byte-swapping; try `hexdump -C`.

lab1_hexedit.c

```
/* Copyright 2009, J Cooperstein coop@coopj.com (GPLv2) */

#include <unistd.h>
#include <fcntl.h>
#include <stdio.h>
#include <stdlib.h>
#include <errno.h>

#define FILE_NAME_DEFAULT "/etc/passwd"
```

```c
#define BYTES_PER_LINE  16

#define DEATH(mess) { perror(mess); exit(errno); }

int main (int argc, char *argv[])
{
    int fd, bytes_read, i;
    unsigned char line[BYTES_PER_LINE];
    char *filename = FILE_NAME_DEFAULT;

    if (argc > 1)
        filename = argv[1];

    printf ("\n **** DISPLAYING (IN HEX) FILE: %s ****\n\n", filename);

    if ((fd = open (filename, O_RDONLY)) < 0)
        DEATH (filename);

    do {
        if ((bytes_read = read (fd, line, BYTES_PER_LINE)) < 0)
            DEATH (filename);

        for (i = 0; i < bytes_read; i++)
            printf ("%2.2x ", line[i]);

        printf ("\n");
    }
    while (bytes_read > 0);

    close (fd);
    exit (0);
}
```

10.2   Lab 2: Files With Offset

- Modify Lab 1 to start that hex display at a file offset specified as a parameter.

lab2_hexedit_offset.c

```c
/* Copyright 2009, J Cooperstein coop@coopj.com (GPLv2) */

#include <unistd.h>
#include <fcntl.h>
#include <stdio.h>
#include <stdlib.h>
#include <errno.h>

#define FILE_NAME_DEFAULT "/etc/passwd"
#define BYTES_PER_LINE  16

#define DEATH(mess) { perror(mess); exit(errno); }
```

```
int main (int argc, char *argv[])
{
    int fd, bytes_read, i, start_addr = 0;
    unsigned char line[BYTES_PER_LINE];
    char *filename = FILE_NAME_DEFAULT;

    if (argc > 1)
        filename = argv[1];

    if (argc > 2)
        start_addr = atoi (argv[2]);

    printf
        ("\n **** DISPLAYING (IN HEX) FILE: %s at offset = %d (=0x%x) ****\n\n",
         filename, start_addr, start_addr);

    if ((fd = open (filename, O_RDONLY)) < 0)
        DEATH (filename);

    if (-1 == lseek (fd, start_addr, SEEK_SET))
        DEATH (filename);

    printf ("starting at 0x%x:\n", start_addr);

    do {
        if ((bytes_read = read (fd, line, BYTES_PER_LINE)) < 0)
            DEATH (filename);

        for (i = 0; i < bytes_read; i++)
            printf ("%2.2x ", line[i]);

        printf ("\n");
    }
    while (bytes_read > 0);

    close (fd);
    exit (0);
}
```

10.3   Lab 3: Using the Standard I/O Library

• Implement the previous lab using the standard I/O library instead of Unix I/O to see the differences.

lab3_stdio.c

```
/* Copyright 2009, J Cooperstein coop@coopj.com (GPLv2) */

#include <stdio.h>
#include <stdlib.h>
#include <errno.h>
```

```
#define FILE_NAME_DEFAULT "/etc/passwd"
#define BYTES_PER_LINE  16

#define DEATH(mess) { perror(mess); exit(errno); }

int main (int argc, char *argv[])
{
    FILE *fp;
    int i = 0, start_addr = 0;
    char c;
    char *filename = FILE_NAME_DEFAULT;

    if (argc > 1)
        filename = argv[1];

    if (argc > 2)
        start_addr = atoi (argv[2]);

    printf
        ("\n **** DISPLAYING (IN HEX) FILE: %s at offset = %d (=0x%x) ****\n\n",
         filename, start_addr, start_addr);

    if (!(fp = fopen (filename, "r")))
        DEATH (filename);

    if (-1 == fseek (fp, start_addr, SEEK_SET))
        DEATH (filename);

    printf ("starting at 0x%x:\n", start_addr);

    while (!feof (fp)) {
        if (fread (&c, 1, 1, fp) < 0)
            DEATH (filename);
        printf ("%2.2x ", c);
        if (i % BYTES_PER_LINE == 0)
            printf ("\n");
        i++;
    }
    printf ("\n");
    fclose (fp);
    exit (0);
}
```

10.4   Lab 4: Using pread() and pwrite()

- Write a program that uses pread() and pwrite(). Obtain the offset within the file using lseek() after each I/O operation and verify that it does not change.

- Using pwrite() fill up a file with distinguishable values depending on position. Then read them back and verify their contents.

lab4_pread.c

```c
/* Copyright 2009, J Cooperstein coop@coopj.com (GPLv2) */
#define _XOPEN_SOURCE 500
#include <unistd.h>
#include <fcntl.h>
#include <stdio.h>
#include <stdlib.h>
#include <errno.h>
#include <string.h>

#define FILE_NAME_DEFAULT "/tmp/junkfile"
#define NVECS 4
#define BLEN 1024

#define DEATH(mess) { perror(mess); exit(errno); }

int main (int argc, char *argv[])
{
    int fd, j;
    char *filename = FILE_NAME_DEFAULT;
    off_t pos;
    char *buf;

    if (argc > 1)
        filename = argv[1];

    buf = malloc (BLEN);

    if ((fd = open (filename, O_RDWR | O_CREAT | O_TRUNC, 0666)) < 0)
        DEATH ("open");

    /* write to the junkfile */

    for (j = 0; j < NVECS; j++) {
        memset (buf, '0' + j, BLEN);
        pos = j * BLEN;
        printf ("Going to write at pos = %d\n", (int)pos);
        pwrite (fd, buf, BLEN, pos);
        pos = lseek (fd, 0, SEEK_CUR);
        printf ("After the %d'th write, the position is %d\n", j, (int)pos);
    }

    /* read from the junkfile */

    for (j = 0; j < NVECS; j++) {
        memset (buf, 0, BLEN);
        pos = j * BLEN;
        printf ("Going to read at pos = %d\n", (int)pos);
        pread (fd, buf, BLEN, pos);
        pos = lseek (fd, 0, SEEK_CUR);
        printf ("After the %d'th read, the position is %d\n", j, (int)pos);
        write (STDOUT_FILENO, buf, BLEN);
        write (STDOUT_FILENO, "\n\n", 2);
    }

    free (buf);
```

```
    close (fd);
    exit (0);
}
```

10.5   Lab 5: Using readv() and writev()

- Write a program that uses readv() and writev().

- Fill up a series of buffers with distinguishable values and write them to a file. Then read them
  back and verify their contents.

lab5_readv.c

```c
/* Copyright 2009, J Cooperstein coop@coopj.com (GPLv2) */

#include <unistd.h>
#include <fcntl.h>
#include <stdio.h>
#include <stdlib.h>
#include <errno.h>
#include <string.h>
#include <ctype.h>
#include <sys/uio.h>

#define FILE_NAME_DEFAULT "/tmp/junkfile"
#define NVECS 4
#define BLEN 1024

#define DEATH(mess) { perror(mess); exit(errno); }

int main (int argc, char *argv[])
{
    int fd, j;
    char *filename = FILE_NAME_DEFAULT;
    struct iovec iov[NVECS];

    if (argc > 1)
        filename = argv[1];

    /* initialize NVECS structures and buffers */

    for (j = 0; j < NVECS; j++) {
        char *buf = malloc (BLEN);
        memset (buf, '0' + j, BLEN);
        iov[j].iov_base = buf;
        iov[j].iov_len = BLEN;
    }

    if ((fd = open (filename, O_RDWR | O_CREAT | O_TRUNC, 0666)) < 0)
        DEATH ("open");

    /* write the buffers out to the junkfile */
```

```
    if (writev (fd, iov, NVECS) < 0)
        DEATH ("writev");

    /* clear out the buffers */

    for (j = 0; j < NVECS; j++) {
        char *buf = iov[j].iov_base;
        memset (buf, 0, BLEN);
    }

    /* reposition to beginning of the file */

    if (-1 == lseek (fd, 0, SEEK_SET))
        DEATH ("lseek");

    /* read the buffers back from the junkfile */

    if (readv (fd, iov, NVECS) < 0)
        DEATH ("readv");

    /* print them out to make sure it wall ok */

    for (j = 0; j < NVECS; j++) {
        write (STDOUT_FILENO, iov[j].iov_base, BLEN);
        write (STDOUT_FILENO, "\n\n", 2);
        free (iov[j].iov_base); /* avoid memory leaks */
    }

    close (fd);
    exit (0);
}
```

Chapter 11

Advanced File Operations

11.1   Lab 1: Directories

- Write a program to search a directory and print out the contents. (In other words, write an **ls** program.)

- **Optional**: Enhance your code to display file permissions in octal, user/group information in decimal, and the size of the file; i.e., mimic the **-l** option to **ls**. You'll have to play with **stat()** to accomplish this.

lab1_ls.c

```
/* Copyright 2009, J Cooperstein coop@coopj.com (GPLv2) */

#include <unistd.h>
#include <sys/types.h>
#include <sys/stat.h>
#include <dirent.h>
#include <stdio.h>
#include <errno.h>
```

```c
#include <stdlib.h>

#define DEATH(mess) { perror(mess); exit(errno); }
#define DIRECTORY_DEF "."

int main (int argc, char *argv[])
{
    DIR *dir;
    struct dirent *direntry;
    char *dirname = DIRECTORY_DEF;
    struct stat info;

    if (argc > 1)
        dirname = argv[1];

    printf ("\n **** DISPLAYING DIRECTORY %s ****\n\n", dirname);

    /* Open the directory */
    if (!(dir = opendir (dirname)))
        DEATH (dirname);

    /* Change to the directory to make stat work if not the current dir */

    if (chdir (dirname))
        DEATH (dirname);

    /* Read each entry in the directory... */
    printf ("   MODE     UID    GID           SIZE\n\n");

    while ((direntry = readdir (dir))) {

        if (stat (direntry->d_name, &info))
            DEATH (" problems fstating the file:");

        printf ("%8o   %4d   %4d   %12d %s\n", info.st_mode,
                info.st_uid, info.st_gid, (int)info.st_size, direntry->d_name);
    }

    /* close the directory */
    closedir (dir);
    exit (0);
}
```

11.2   Lab 2: Memory Mapping

- Write a program that uses mmap to access a file.

- Have the program both read and write to the file using memory access rather than read/write
  functions. (Make sure you work on a file you don't care about!)

lab2_mmap.c

/* Copyright 2009, J Cooperstein coop@coopj.com (GPLv2) */

```
#include <stdlib.h>
#include <stdio.h>
#include <unistd.h>
#include <string.h>
#include <fcntl.h>
#include <errno.h>
#include <sys/mman.h>
#include <sys/stat.h>
#include <sys/types.h>

#define DEATH(mess) { perror(mess); exit(errno); }

int main (int argc, char **argv)
{
    int fd, size, rc, j;
    char *area, *tmp;
    struct stat filestat;
    char c[2] = "CX";

    if ((fd = open (argv[1], O_RDWR)) < 0)
        DEATH ("problems opening the file");

    if (fstat (fd, &filestat))
        DEATH (" problems fstating the file:");

    size = filestat.st_size;
    printf (" Memory Mapping File: %s, of size %d bytes\n", argv[1], size);

    area = mmap (NULL, size, PROT_WRITE | PROT_READ, MAP_SHARED, fd, 0);

    if (area == MAP_FAILED)
        DEATH ("error mmaping");

    /* can close the file now */

    close (fd);

    /* put the string repeatedly in the file */

    tmp = area;
    for (j = 0; j < size - 1; j += 2, tmp += 2)
        memcpy (tmp, &c, 2);

    /* just cat out the file to see if it worked */

    rc = write (STDOUT_FILENO, area, size);

    if (rc != size)
        DEATH ("problems writing");

    exit (0);
}
```

11.3   Lab 3: Symbolic links

- Write a program to search a directory for symbolic links.

- If it finds any, check to see if the link is valid or broken.

lab3_symlink.c

```c
/* Copyright 2009, J Cooperstein coop@coopj.com (GPLv2) */

#include <unistd.h>
#include <sys/types.h>
#include <sys/stat.h>
#include <dirent.h>
#include <stdio.h>
#include <string.h>
#include <stdlib.h>
#include <errno.h>

#define DEATH(mess) { perror(mess); exit(errno); }

#define DIRECTORY_DEF "/"
#define MAXPATH 256

int main (int argc, char *argv[])
{
    DIR *dir;
    struct dirent *direntry;
    struct stat file_info;
    char filename[MAXPATH], filename2[MAXPATH];
    char *dirname = DIRECTORY_DEF;

    if (argc > 1)
        dirname = argv[1];

    if (chdir (dirname))
        DEATH (dirname);

    if (!(dir = opendir ("./")))
        DEATH (dirname);

    /* Read each entry in the directory... */

    while ((direntry = readdir (dir))) {
        strcpy (filename, direntry->d_name);

        if (lstat (filename, &file_info))
            fprintf (stderr, "Error lstating %s\n", filename);

        /* ...if it's a link, find the other end. */

        else if (S_ISLNK (file_info.st_mode)) {

            memset (filename2, 0, sizeof (filename2));
```

```
            if (-1 == readlink (filename, filename2, sizeof (filename2))) {
                printf ("failed using readlink\n");

            } else {

                if (lstat (filename2, &file_info))
                    printf ("%s is a broken link to %s\n", filename, filename2);
                else
                    printf ("%s is a link to %s\n", filename, filename2);
            }
        }
    }
    closedir (dir);
    exit (0);
}
```

11.4   Lab 4: File locking

- Write a program to examine file locking.

- Arguments may be specified on the command line or from an input file, which say whether the lock should be exclusive or not, whether it should be read or write, and what region of the file (or the whole file) it should apply to.

- Run more than one instance of the program simultaneously to examine what happens.

lab4_lock.c

```
/* Copyright 2009, J Cooperstein coop@coopj.com (GPLv2) */

#include <unistd.h>
#include <stdio.h>
#include <string.h>
#include <sys/fcntl.h>
#include <stdlib.h>
#include <errno.h>

#define DEATH(mess) { perror(mess); exit(errno); }

struct flock mylock;

int main (int argc, char *argv[])
{
    int fd, cmd, flags, rc;

    pid_t pid;
    char *filename, *which;

    flags = O_RDWR;
    pid = getpid ();
    mylock.l_type = F_RDLCK;
```

```
    if (argc < 3) {
        printf ("USAGE: %s filename {r:w}\n", argv[0]);
        exit (-1);
    }
    filename = argv[1];
    which = argv[2];

    if ((fd = open (filename, flags)) < 0)
        DEATH (filename);

    printf ("\nPID=%d, Opening: %s, with fd = %d\n", pid, filename, fd);

    cmd = F_GETLK;
    rc = fcntl (fd, cmd, &mylock);
    printf ("\nPID=%d, F_GETLK returns rc=%d:\n", pid, rc);
    printf
        ("     l_type=%d, l_whence=%d, l_start=%d, l_len=%d, l_pid=%d\n\n",
         mylock.l_type, mylock.l_whence, (int)mylock.l_start,
         (int)mylock.l_len, mylock.l_pid);

    cmd = F_SETLK;

    if (!strncmp (which, "r", 1)) {
        mylock.l_type = F_RDLCK;
        printf ("PID=%d, doing F_RDLCK\n", pid);
    } else {
        mylock.l_type = F_WRLCK;
        printf ("PID=%d, doing F_WRLCK\n", pid);
    }

    rc = fcntl (fd, cmd, &mylock);
    mylock.l_len = 0;
    printf ("PID=%d, F_SETLK returns rc=%d:\n", pid, rc);
    printf
        ("     l_type=%d, l_whence=%d, l_start=%d, l_len=%d, l_pid=%d\n\n",
         mylock.l_type, mylock.l_whence, (int)mylock.l_start,
         (int)mylock.l_len, mylock.l_pid);

    sleep (6);
    printf (" PID=%d is done sleeping 6 seconds \n", pid);
    exit (0);

}
```

11.5   Lab 5: Making Temporary Files

- Write a program that uses `mkstemp()` and `tmpfile()` to create and open temporary files, and `mkdtemp()` for a directory.

- While the program is running (you can use `sleep()` do induce a delay) verify the files are created and check their names against the template for `mkstemp()`, `mkdtemp()`. For `tmpnam()` you may want to run your program under **strace** to see what is really happening.

lab5_tmp.c

```c
/* Copyright 2009, J Cooperstein coop@coopj.com (GPLv2) */

#include <stdlib.h>
#include <stdio.h>
#include <unistd.h>

int main ()
{
    int fd;
    FILE *fp;
    char *f_mkdtemp;
    char template_file[] = "AAXXXXXX", template_dir[] = "BBXXXXXX";

    printf ("template_file = %s\n", template_file);
    fd = mkstemp (template_file);
    printf ("template_file = %s\n", template_file);

    f_mkdtemp = mkdtemp (template_dir);

    printf ("f_mkdtemp = %s template_dir=%s\n", f_mkdtemp, template_dir);

    fp = tmpfile ();
    sleep (10);
    unlink (template_file);
    rmdir (f_mkdtemp);
    exit (0);
}
```

11.6   Lab 6: Using inotify to Monitor a Directory

- Use **inotify** to monitory changes to the **/tmp** directory.

- When reading events check the bits in the returned mask to see what kinds of events have occurred, when you create files, remove them, read them, change their attributes, etc.

- You man want to consult the **man** page for **inotify** to get a complete list of event bits.

lab6_inotify.c

```c
/* Copyright 2009, J Cooperstein coop@coopj.com (GPLv2) */

#include <unistd.h>
#include <stdlib.h>
#include <stdio.h>
#include <errno.h>
#include <sys/inotify.h>
#include <string.h>

#define checkfor(m, a, s) if (ev->mask & a) printf("mask includes %s\n", s);
```

```c
int main (int argc, char *argv[])
{
    int fd, nb, offset, bufsize;
    char *buf;
    struct inotify_event *ev;

    bufsize = getpagesize ();
    buf = malloc (bufsize);
    printf ("sizeof inotify_event = %ld\n", sizeof (struct inotify_event));
    fd = inotify_init ();
    printf ("fd from inotify_init=%d\n", fd);
    printf ("inotify_add_watch=%d\n",
            inotify_add_watch (fd, "/tmp", IN_ALL_EVENTS));

    for (;;) {
        offset = 0;
        memset (buf, 0, bufsize);
        nb = read (fd, buf, bufsize);
        printf ("\nnb from read=%d\n\n", nb);
        while (offset < nb) {
            ev = (struct inotify_event *)(buf + offset);

            printf ("Event: wd=%d, mask=%0x, cookie=%d, len=%4d, name=%s\n",
                    ev->wd, ev->mask, ev->cookie, ev->len, ev->name);
            checkfor (ev->mask, IN_ACCESS, "IN_ACCESS");
            checkfor (ev->mask, IN_ATTRIB, "IN_ATTRIB");
            checkfor (ev->mask, IN_CLOSE_WRITE, "IN_CLOSE_WRITE");
            checkfor (ev->mask, IN_CLOSE_NOWRITE, "IN_CLOSE_NOWRITE");
            checkfor (ev->mask, IN_CREATE, "IN_CREATE");
            checkfor (ev->mask, IN_DELETE, "IN_DELETE");
            checkfor (ev->mask, IN_DELETE_SELF, "IN_DELETE_SELF");
            checkfor (ev->mask, IN_MODIFY, "IN_MODIFY");
            checkfor (ev->mask, IN_MOVE_SELF, "IN_MOVE_SELF");
            checkfor (ev->mask, IN_MOVED_FROM, "IN_MOVED_FROM");
            checkfor (ev->mask, IN_MOVED_TO, "IN_MOVED_TO");
            checkfor (ev->mask, IN_OPEN, "IN_OPEN");
            offset += sizeof (struct inotify_event) + ev->len;
        }
    }
    exit (0);
}
```

Chapter 12

Processes - I

12.1   Lab 1: Getting and Setting Limits

- Write a user-space program that examines and sets usage limits, and reports statistics on total usage.

- The program should first obtain and print out the current usage limits.

- It should then modify one or more of them, and then print out the new limits.

- The program should give birth to several children using `fork()`, each of which should print out their usage limits, compare to those of the parent and then sleep for a while. The parent should **wait** for the children using `wait()` or `waitpid()`.

- Have the parent use the `getrusage()` function to obtain statistics both for itself and for the children.

`lab1_limit.c`

```c
#include <sys/time.h>
#include <sys/resource.h>
#include <unistd.h>
#include <stdlib.h>
#include <stdio.h>
#include <sys/wait.h>
#include <errno.h>

#define DEATH(mess) { perror(mess); exit(errno); }

void do_limit (int limit, const char *limit_string, struct rlimit *rlim)
{
    if (getrlimit (limit, rlim))
        fprintf (stderr, "Failed in getrlimit\n");
    printf ("%15s=%2d: cur=%20lu,      max=%20lu\n", limit_string,
            limit, rlim->rlim_cur, rlim->rlim_max);
}

void print_limits (void)
{
    struct rlimit rlim;
    do_limit (RLIMIT_CPU, "RLIMIT_CPU", &rlim);
    do_limit (RLIMIT_FSIZE, "RLMIT_FSIZE", &rlim);
    do_limit (RLIMIT_DATA, "RLMIT_DATA", &rlim);
    do_limit (RLIMIT_STACK, "RLIMIT_STACK", &rlim);
    do_limit (RLIMIT_CORE, "RLIMIT_CORE", &rlim);
    do_limit (RLIMIT_RSS, "RLIMIT_RSS", &rlim);
    do_limit (RLIMIT_NPROC, "RLIMIT_NPROC", &rlim);
    do_limit (RLIMIT_NOFILE, "RLIMIT_NOFILE", &rlim);
    do_limit (RLIMIT_MEMLOCK, "RLIMIT_MEMLOCK", &rlim);
    do_limit (RLIMIT_AS, "RLIMIT_AS", &rlim);
    do_limit (RLIMIT_LOCKS, "RLIMIT_LOCKS", &rlim);
}

void print_rusage (int who)
{
    struct rusage usage;
    if (getrusage (who, &usage))
        DEATH ("getrusage failed");

    if (who == RUSAGE_SELF)
        printf ("For RUSAGE_SELF\n");
    if (who == RUSAGE_CHILDREN)
        printf ("\nFor RUSAGE_CHILDREN\n");

    printf
        ("ru_utime.tv_sec, ru_utime.tv_usec = %4d  %4d (user time used)\n",
         (int)usage.ru_utime.tv_sec, (int)usage.ru_utime.tv_usec);
    printf
        ("ru_stime.tv_sec, ru_stime.tv_usec = %4d  %4d (system time used)\n",
         (int)usage.ru_stime.tv_sec, (int)usage.ru_stime.tv_usec);
    printf ("ru_maxrss = %4ld (max resident set size)\n", usage.ru_maxrss);
    printf ("ru_ixrss =  %4ld (integral shared memory size)\n",
            usage.ru_ixrss);
    printf ("ru_idrss =   %4ld (integral unshared data size)\n",
```

```
                  usage.ru_idrss);
    printf ("ru_isrss =    %4ld (integral unshared stack size)\n",
                  usage.ru_isrss);
    printf ("ru_minflt =  %4ld (page reclaims)\n", usage.ru_minflt);
    printf ("ru_majflt =  %4ld (page faults)\n", usage.ru_majflt);
    printf ("ru_nswap =    %4ld (swaps)\n", usage.ru_nswap);
    printf ("ru_inblock = %4ld (block input operations)\n", usage.ru_inblock);
    printf ("ru_oublock = %4ld (block output operations)\n", usage.ru_oublock);
    printf ("ru_msgsnd =  %4ld (messages sent)\n", usage.ru_msgsnd);
    printf ("ru_msgrcv =  %4ld (messages received)\n", usage.ru_msgrcv);
    printf ("ru_nsignals= %4ld (signals received)\n", usage.ru_nsignals);
    printf ("ru_nvcsw=    %4ld (voluntary context switches)\n", usage.ru_nvcsw);
    printf ("ru_nivcsw=   %4ld (involuntary context switches)\n",
                  usage.ru_nivcsw);
}

int main (int argc, char *argv[])
{
    struct rlimit rlim;
    pid_t pid = 0;
    int status = 0, nchildren = 3, i;

    /* Print out all limits */

    printf ("Printing out all limits for pid=%d:\n", getpid ());
    print_limits ();

    /* change and printout the limit for core file size */

    printf ("\nBefore Modification, this is RLIMIT_CORE:\n");
    do_limit (RLIMIT_CORE, "RLIMIT_CORE", &rlim);
    rlim.rlim_cur = 8 * 1024 * 1024;
    printf ("I forked off a child with pid = %d\n", (int)pid);

    setrlimit (RLIMIT_CORE, &rlim);
    printf ("\nAfter  Modification, this is RLIMIT_CORE:\n");
    do_limit (RLIMIT_CORE, "RLIMIT_CORE", &rlim);

    /* fork off the nchildren */

    fflush (stdout);
    for (i = 0; i < nchildren; i++) {
        pid = fork ();
        if (pid < 0)
            DEATH ("Failed in fork");
        if (pid == 0) {          /* any child */
            printf ("\nIn child pid= %d this is RLIMIT_CORE:\n",
                    (int)getpid ());
            do_limit (RLIMIT_CORE, "RLIMIT_CORE", &rlim);
            fflush (stdout);
            sleep (3);
            exit (0);
        }
    }
```

```
    while (pid > 0) {              /* parent */
        pid = wait (&status);
        printf ("Parent got return on pid=%dn\n", (int)pid);
    }

    printf (" ***************************************************** \n");
    print_rusage (RUSAGE_SELF);
    print_rusage (RUSAGE_CHILDREN);

    exit (0);
}
```

12.2   Lab 2: Process Groups

- Write a program that first prints out its process group using both getpgid() and getpgrp().

- Then feeding as an argument to the program the process ID of a currently running process (you could simply do cat & and use the echoed process ID as an argument) print out the **pgid** of the process.

- Now try to change it with setpgid() to be the same as that of your program. Read the **man** page to understand your results.

lab2_pgid.c

```
/* Copyright 2009, J Cooperstein coop@coopj.com (GPLv2) */

#define _XOPEN_SOURCE 500

#include <unistd.h>
#include <stdio.h>
#include <sys/types.h>
#include <sys/wait.h>
#include <stdlib.h>
#include <errno.h>

int main (int argc, char *argv[])
{
    pid_t mypid, pid;
    int rc;

    /* print information about myself */

    mypid = getpid ();
    printf ("pgroup from getpgid(pid) = %d\n", getpgid (mypid));
    printf ("pgroup from getpgrp() = %d\n", getpgrp ());

    if (argc < 2)
        exit (EXIT_FAILURE);
    if ((pid = atoi (argv[1])) < 0) {
        printf (" give a running pid as an argument\n");
        exit (EXIT_FAILURE);
    }
```

```
    printf ("pgroup for pid=%d = %d\n", pid, getpgid (pid));

    /* try to change the pgroup to my group */

    rc = setpgid (pid, mypid);
    printf ("rc from setpgid(pid,mypid)= %d\n", rc);
    printf ("pgroup for pid=%d = %d\n", pid, getpgid (pid));
    exit (EXIT_SUCCESS);
}
```

12.3 Lab 3: The proc filesystem

- Find a process on your system that uses multiple threads. A good candidate would be **firefox**.
  To gain information about the process you can do:

```
$ ps -eLF  | grep -e PID -e firef
UID      PID  PPID   LWP  C NLWP    SZ   RSS PSR STIME TTY        TIME CMD
coop    4889     1  4889  0    1 15970  1228   1 07:16 ?      00:00:00 /bin/sh /usr/lib64/
                                                                       firefox-3.0.15/run-moz
coop    4914  4889  4914  2    7 185029 257084 0 07:16 ?      00:11:38 /usr/lib64/firefox-
coop    4914  4889  4948  0    7 185029 257084 0 07:16 ?      00:00:02 /usr/lib64/firefox-
coop    4914  4889  4949  0    7 185029 257084 0 07:16 ?      00:00:17 /usr/lib64/firefox-
coop    4914  4889  4963  0    7 185029 257084 3 07:16 ?      00:00:00 /usr/lib64/firefox-
coop    4914  4889  4964  0    7 185029 257084 3 07:16 ?      00:00:00 /usr/lib64/firefox-
coop    4914  4889  4965  0    7 185029 257084 3 07:16 ?      00:00:00 /usr/lib64/firefox-
coop    4914  4889 16800  0    7 185029 257084 2 09:42 ?      00:00:00 /usr/lib64/firefox-
coop   25769  4567 25769  0    1 15302   808   3 16:27 pts/1  00:00:00 grep -e PID -e firef
```

- Note the second process listed has 7 **LWP**'s (light weight processes, or threads) associated with
  it. If you examine the associated subdirectory in the **proc** filesystem (**/proc/4914** in the above
  example) you will find a subdirectory under the **tasks** subdirectory for each process.

- While you are there take a good look at the entries in the subdirectories, some of which we will
  discuss later.

lab2_pgid.c

```
/* Copyright 2009, J Cooperstein coop@coopj.com (GPLv2) */

#define _XOPEN_SOURCE 500

#include <unistd.h>
#include <stdio.h>
#include <sys/types.h>
#include <sys/wait.h>
#include <stdlib.h>
#include <errno.h>

int main (int argc, char *argv[])
{
    pid_t mypid, pid;
    int rc;
```

```c
    /* print information about myself */

    mypid = getpid ();
    printf ("pgroup from getpgid(pid) = %d\n", getpgid (mypid));
    printf ("pgroup from getpgrp() = %d\n", getpgrp ());

    if (argc < 2)
        exit (EXIT_FAILURE);
    if ((pid = atoi (argv[1])) < 0) {
        printf (" give a running pid as an argument\n");
        exit (EXIT_FAILURE);
    }
    printf ("pgroup for pid=%d = %d\n", pid, getpgid (pid));

    /* try to change the pgroup to my group */

    rc = setpgid (pid, mypid);
    printf ("rc from setpgid(pid,mypid)= %d\n", rc);
    printf ("pgroup for pid=%d = %d\n", pid, getpgid (pid));
    exit (EXIT_SUCCESS);
}
```

Chapter 13

Processes - II

13.1 Lab 1: Forking

- Write a simple forking example:

- Parent and child must be able to identify themselves as to which is which.

- The parent should `wait` for the child to terminate.

lab1_fork.c

```
/* Copyright 2009, J Cooperstein coop@coopj.com (GPLv2) */

#include <stdio.h>
#include <unistd.h>
#include <sys/types.h>
#include <sys/wait.h>
#include <stdlib.h>
#include <errno.h>

#define DEATH(mess) { perror(mess); exit(errno); }
```

```
int main (int argc, char *argv[])
{
    int wait_stat;
    pid_t pid, ch_pid;

    printf ("\nThis is the parent, about to fork. pid=%d\n", getpid ());
    fflush (stdout);
    pid = fork ();

    if (pid > 0) {
        printf ("\nThis is the parent, after the fork. Child pid=%d\n", pid);
        ch_pid = wait (&wait_stat);
        if (WIFEXITED (wait_stat))
            printf ("\nChild exited with code %d\n", WEXITSTATUS (wait_stat));
        else
            printf ("\nChild terminated abnormally\n");
        exit (EXIT_SUCCESS);
    }
    if (pid == 0) {
        printf ("\nThis is the child, after the fork. pid=%d\n", getpid ());
        exit (EXIT_SUCCESS);
    }
    DEATH ("fork");
}
```

13.2   Lab 2: Zombie Limescale

- Modify the previous forking program so that the child terminates quickly, while the parent hibernates for a period of time with sleep().

- Run the program in one terminal window (or in background with &) while monitoring your active processes with ps ux, noting the state of the child. The child should disappear when the parent exits.

lab2_zombie.c

```
/* Copyright 2009, J Cooperstein coop@coopj.com (GPLv2) */

#include <stdio.h>
#include <unistd.h>
#include <sys/types.h>
#include <sys/wait.h>
#include <stdlib.h>
#include <errno.h>

#define DEATH(mess) { perror(mess); exit(errno); }

int main (int argc, char *argv[])
{
    pid_t pid;
```

```
    printf ("\nThis is the parent, about to fork. pid=%d\n", getpid ());
    fflush (stdout);
    pid = fork ();

    if (pid > 0) {
        printf ("\nThis is the parent, after the fork. Child pid=%d\n", pid);
        sleep(10);
        printf ("\nThis is the parent waking up and exiting\n");
        exit (EXIT_SUCCESS);
    }
    if (pid == 0) {
        printf ("\nThis is the child, after the fork. pid=%d\n", getpid ());
        exit (EXIT_SUCCESS);
    }
    DEATH ("fork");
}
```

13.3   Lab 3: More Forking and Waiting

- Modify your **ls** program from the previous section so that, for every subdirectory found (you can use stat() and S_ISDIR() to detect directories), it forks a child to process that subdirectory (you probably want to skip processing . and ..).

- If the output gets too muddled, you can have the parent wait() for each child to finish.

- It is possible to create too many processes and hang your machine. See help ulimit and type ulimit -a to get the current limits. Set the maximum number of processes to a reasonable value.

lab3_ls.c

```
/* Copyright 2009, J Cooperstein coop@coopj.com (GPLv2) */

#include <stdio.h>
#include <unistd.h>
#include <sys/types.h>
#include <sys/stat.h>
#include <sys/wait.h>
#include <dirent.h>
#include <errno.h>
#include <string.h>
#include <stdlib.h>

#define DIRECTORY_DEF "."
#define DEATH(mess) { perror(mess); exit(errno); }

void process_dir (char *this_dir);

int main (int argc, char *argv[])
{
    char *dirname = DIRECTORY_DEF;
```

```
    if (argc > 1)
        dirname = argv[1];
    printf ("DIRECTORY: %s - %d\n", dirname, getpid ());
    process_dir (dirname);
    exit (EXIT_SUCCESS);
}

void process_dir (char *this_dir)
{
    DIR *dir;
    struct dirent *direntry;
    struct stat file_info;
    int status;

    if (chdir (this_dir))
        DEATH (this_dir);

    if (!(dir = opendir ("./")))
        DEATH (this_dir);

    /* List all directory entries */

    while ((direntry = readdir (dir))) {
        if (lstat (direntry->d_name, &file_info))
            fprintf (stderr, "Error lstat()ing %s\n", direntry->d_name);
        printf ("    %d:  %s\n", getpid (), direntry->d_name);
    }

    /* rewind and then recurse through subdirectories */

    rewinddir (dir);

    while ((direntry = readdir (dir))) {

        if (lstat (direntry->d_name, &file_info))
            fprintf (stderr, "Error lstat()ing %s\n", direntry->d_name);

        /* ...if it's a directory.... */
        else if (S_ISDIR (file_info.st_mode)) {

            pid_t pid;

            /* don't do it if it is . or .. */

            if (strcmp (direntry->d_name, ".") &&
                strcmp (direntry->d_name, "..")) {

                fflush (stdout);
                pid = fork ();
                if (pid == 0) {
                    printf ("\nPID  %d DIRECTORY: %s\n",
                            getpid (), direntry->d_name);
                    process_dir (direntry->d_name);
                    exit (EXIT_SUCCESS);
                }
```

```
                    if (pid > 0)
                        wait (&status);
                    else
                        DEATH ("fork failed");


                }                       /* not . or .. */
            }                           /* directory */
        }                               /* while direntry */
    closedir (dir);
}
```

13.4   Lab 4: Cloning

- Write a short program that uses the clone() system call to create master and slave threads that share all memory resources.

- Have a global variable and show that either thread can modify it and the value can be seen by the other.

- Be careful with creation of the slave thread's stack pointer, to point to the top of the stack since it grows down.

- What happens if the slave thread dies before the master thread?

- Note you can use this as a nucleus of your own multi-threaded programming method that does not use the standard threading libraries. You can also play with sharing file descriptors or not etc.

lab4_clone.c

```
/* Copyright 2009, J Cooperstein coop@coopj.com (GPLv2) */

#include <sched.h>
#include <signal.h>
#include <stdio.h>
#include <stdlib.h>
#include <unistd.h>
#include <malloc.h>
#include <sys/types.h>
#include <sys/wait.h>

int param = 0;

int slav (void *data)
{
    int j;
    printf ("starting off slave thread, pid=%d\n", getpid ());
    for (j = 0; j < 10; j++) {
        param = j + 1000;
        sleep (1);
        printf ("\nslave thread running: j=%d, param=%d secs\n", j, param);
    }
    printf ("\nSlave thread saying goodbye\n");
```

```
        return 0;
}

int main (int argc, char **argv)
{
    int j, tid, pagesize, stacksize;
    void *stack;

    printf ("starting off master thread, pid=%d\n", getpid ());

    pagesize = getpagesize ();
    stacksize = 4 * pagesize;

    /* could probably just use malloc(), but this is safer */
    /* stack = (char *)memalign (pagesize, stacksize); */
    posix_memalign (&stack, pagesize, stacksize);

    printf ("Setting off a clone thread with stacksize = %d....", stacksize);
    tid = clone (slav, (char *)stack + stacksize - 1, CLONE_VM | SIGCHLD, 0);
    printf (" with tid=%d\n", tid);
    if (tid < 0)
        exit (1);

    /* could do a  wait (&status) here if required */

    for (j = 0; j < 6; j++) {
        param = j;
        sleep (1);
        printf ("\nmaster thread running: j=%d, param=%d secs\n", j, param);
    }
    printf ("master killitself\n");
    free (stack);
    exit (0);
}
```

13.5   Lab 5: Exiting

- Have a program use atexit() (or on_exit()), or the constructor/destructor methods for exit handling..

- Register at least two handlers to be processed during exiting.

- Can you make what happens depend on the exit code from your main routine?

lab5_atexit.c

```
 /* Copyright 2009, J Cooperstein coop@coopj.com (GPLv2) */

#include <stdlib.h>
#include <stdio.h>
#include <errno.h>

#define DEATH(mess) { perror(mess); exit(errno); }
```

```
void my_atexit_fun1 (void)
{
    printf ("I am in my_atexit_fun1\n");
}

void my_atexit_fun2 (void)
{
    printf ("I am in my_atexit_fun2\n");
}

int main (int argc, char *argv[])
{
    printf ("beginning the atexit program .... \n");

    if (atexit (my_atexit_fun1) < 0)
        DEATH ("atexit");
    printf ("Installed my_atexit_fun1\n");

    if (atexit (my_atexit_fun2) < 0)
        DEATH ("atexit");
    printf ("Installed my_atexit_fun2\n");

    exit (EXIT_SUCCESS);
}
```

lab5_onexit.c

```
/* Copyright 2009, J Cooperstein coop@coopj.com (GPLv2) */

#include <stdlib.h>
#include <stdio.h>
#include <errno.h>

#define DEATH(mess) { perror(mess); exit(errno); }

void my_on_exit_fun (int rc_exit, int *arg)
{
    printf ("I am in my_on_exit_fun, rc_exit = %d, arg = %d\n", rc_exit, *arg);
}

int main (int argc, char *argv[])
{
    int exit_code, arg1 = 1;

    if (argc > 1) {
        exit_code = atoi (argv[1]);
    } else {
        printf (" USAGE: %s exit_code\n", argv[0]);
        exit (-1);
    }

    printf ("beginning the on_exit program: \n");
    if (on_exit ((void *)my_on_exit_fun, &arg1) < 0)
        DEATH ("on_exit");
```

```
    printf ("Installed  my_on_exit_fun\n");

    exit (exit_code);
}
```

lab5_decon.c

```
/* Copyright 2009, J Cooperstein coop@coopj.com (GPLv2) */

#include <stdlib.h>
#include <stdio.h>
#include <errno.h>

void exit_fun1 (void) __attribute__ ((destructor));
void exit_fun2 (void) __attribute__ ((destructor));

void exit_fun1 (void)
{
    printf ("I am in exit_fun1\n");
}

void exit_fun2 (void)
{
    printf ("I am in exit_fun2\n");
}

int main (int argc, char *argv[])
{
    printf ("About to call exit from %s program .... \n", argv[0]);
    exit (0);
}
```

13.6   Lab 6: Memory Mapping

- Write a program that uses **anonymous** memory mapping for parent/child communication.

- Have the child write to the memory mapped region and have the parent read from it.

lab6_mmap.c

```
/* Copyright 2009, J Cooperstein coop@coopj.com (GPLv2) */
#include <stdlib.h>
#include <stdio.h>
#include <unistd.h>
#include <string.h>
#include <sys/mman.h>
#include <sys/types.h>
#include <sys/wait.h>

int main (int argc, char **argv)
{
    int fd = -1, size = 4096, status;
```

```
    char *area;
    pid_t pid;

    area =
        mmap (NULL, size, PROT_READ | PROT_WRITE, MAP_SHARED | MAP_ANONYMOUS,
            fd, 0);

    pid = fork ();
    if (pid == 0) {                 /* child */
        strcpy (area, "This is a message from the child");
        printf ("Child has written: %s\n", area);
        exit (EXIT_SUCCESS);
    }
    if (pid > 0) {                  /* parent */
        wait (&status);
        printf ("Parent has read:   %s\n", area);
        exit (EXIT_SUCCESS);
    }
    exit (EXIT_FAILURE);
}
```

13.7   Lab 7: Daemons

- Write a simple program that starts a daemon process. It can be as simple as just calling pause() to go to sleep until a signal is received.

- Once the program is running, type ps 1x to verify it is running in background and that its parent process is **init**

- Send a signal to the daemon to interrupt the sleep; for instance one could do kill -SIGUSR1 <pid>. The process should disappear.

lab7_daemon.c

```
/* Copyright 2009, J Cooperstein coop@coopj.com (GPLv2) */

#include <unistd.h>
#include <stdio.h>
#include <stdlib.h>

int main ()
{
    daemon (0, 0);
    pause ();
    printf ("got out of the pause\n");
    exit (0);
}
```

Chapter 14

Pipes and Fifos

14.1   Lab 1: pipe - parent/child with exec

- Change the parent/child lab example have the child `exec()` a command (say an `ls -l /usr/bin`) and stuff it into the pipe, and have the parent read the output from the pipe and display it.

- Do this using only the `pipe()`, call, and not the `popen()` call.

lab1_pchild_exec.c

```
/* Copyright 2009, J Cooperstein coop@coopj.com (GPLv2) */

#include <stdio.h>
#include <unistd.h>
#include <stdlib.h>
#include <errno.h>
#include <sys/wait.h>

#define DEATH(mess) { perror(mess); exit(errno); }
```

```
int main (int argc, char *argv[])
{
    pid_t pid;
    int rc, filedes[2], BSIZE=getpagesize();
    char *buffer = malloc (BSIZE);
    char *dirname = "/usr/bin";

    if (-1 == pipe (filedes))
        DEATH ("pipe");
    if (argc > 1)
        dirname = argv[1];

    printf ("\nThis is the parent, about to fork\n");
    fflush (stdout);
    pid = fork ();

    if (pid > 0) {
        printf ("\nThis is the parent, after the fork\n");
        close (filedes[1]);

        /* Read (blocking) from the pipe until it goes away. */
        printf ("\nThe parent just read the following from the pipe:\n");
        while ((rc = read (filedes[0], buffer, BSIZE)) > 0)
            write (STDOUT_FILENO, buffer, rc);

        exit (EXIT_SUCCESS);
    }
    if (pid == 0) {
        printf ("\nThis is the child, after the fork\n");
        dup2 (STDOUT_FILENO, filedes[1]);
        /* could also do:
           close (STDOUT_FILENO);
           dup (filedes[1]);
         */
        close (filedes[0]);
        execlp ("ls", "ls", "-l", dirname, NULL);
        exit (EXIT_FAILURE);
    }
    DEATH ("fork");
}
```

14.2   Lab 2: popen/pclose

- Modify the previous lab to have the child use popen()/pclose().

lab2_popen.c

```
/* Copyright 2009, J Cooperstein coop@coopj.com (GPLv2) */

#include <stdio.h>
#include <unistd.h>
#include <stdlib.h>
```

```c
#include <errno.h>
#include <string.h>

#define DEATH(mess) { perror(mess); exit(errno); }

int main (int argc, char *argv[])
{
    pid_t pid;
    char *dirname = "/usr/bin";
    int rc, filedes[2], BSIZE=getpagesize();
    char *buffer = malloc(BSIZE);

    if (-1 == pipe (filedes))
        DEATH ("pipe");
    if (argc > 1)
        dirname = argv[1];

    printf ("\nThis is the parent, about to fork\n");
    fflush (stdout);
    pid = fork ();

    if (pid > 0) {
        printf ("\nThis is the parent, after the fork\n");
        close (filedes[1]);

        /* Read (blocking) from the pipe until it goes away. */
        printf ("\nThe parent just read the following from the pipe:\n");
        while ((rc = read (filedes[0], buffer, BSIZE)) > 0)
            write (STDOUT_FILENO, buffer, rc);

        exit (EXIT_SUCCESS);
    }

    if (pid == 0) {
        FILE *cmd_fd;
        char cmd[1024] = "ls -l ";

        printf ("\nThis is the child, after the fork\n");
        close (filedes[0]);
        cmd_fd = popen (strcat (cmd, dirname), "r");

        while ((rc = fread (buffer, 1, BSIZE, cmd_fd)) > 0)
            write (filedes[1], buffer, rc);

        pclose (cmd_fd);
        exit (EXIT_SUCCESS);
    }
    DEATH ("fork");
}
```

14.3   Lab 3: FIFO's

- Have your program create a node using `mkfifo()` or `mknod()` function call. Fork and then have the child stuff a message in the FIFO and have the parent read it and print it out.

lab3_fifo.c

```c
/* Copyright 2009, J Cooperstein coop@coopj.com (GPLv2) */

#include <stdio.h>
#include <unistd.h>
#include <fcntl.h>
#include <stdlib.h>
#include <errno.h>
#include <sys/types.h>
#include <sys/stat.h>
#include <sys/wait.h>

#define DEATH(mess) { perror(mess); exit(errno); }
#define FIFO_NAME "/tmp/myfifo"

int main (int argc, char *argv[])
{
    char message[] = "Hello World on a FIFO";
    int fd;
    pid_t pid;

    if (mkfifo (FIFO_NAME, 0666) < 0)
        DEATH (FIFO_NAME);

    printf ("FIFO created: %s\n", FIFO_NAME);

    fflush (stdout);
    pid = fork ();

    if (pid == 0) {
        /* child */
        fd = open (FIFO_NAME, O_WRONLY);
        printf ("The child is sending: %s ***\n", message);

        if (write (fd, message, sizeof (message)) < 0)
            DEATH ("write error from child to fifo");

        close (fd);
        exit (EXIT_SUCCESS);
    }

    if (pid > 0) {
        /* parent */
        fd = open (FIFO_NAME, O_RDONLY);
        if (read (fd, message, sizeof (message)) < 0)
            DEATH ("read error in parent from fifo");

        printf ("The parent received: %s ***\n", message);
```

```
            close (fd);

            if (unlink (FIFO_NAME))
                DEATH ("Had trouble removing fifo");

            exit (EXIT_SUCCESS);
        }

    DEATH ("fork");
}
```

14.4   Lab 4: Using splice()

- Write a program that reads data from an input file and transfers it to an output pipe using splice().

- By default the program should do it all in one system call. As an optional argument give the number of bytes that should be done in one transfer and loop until the total is consumed.

- Create a fifo as the output pipe and then run your program in one window, while doing cat < afifo in another. Try starting the **cat** before and after your program runs.

lab4_splice.c

```
/* Copyright 2009, J. Cooperstein coop@coopj.com (GPLv2) */
#define _GNU_SOURCE

#include <stdio.h>
#include <stdlib.h>
#include <unistd.h>
#include <fcntl.h>
#include <string.h>
#include <limits.h>
#include <errno.h>

#define DEATH(mess) { perror(mess); exit(errno); }

int main (int argc, char *argv[])
{
    char infile[128] = "./infile", outpipe[128] = "./outpipe";
    int rc, fd_in, fd_out, nbuf = INT_MAX;

    /* 1st arg = infilename       (./infile by default)
       2nd arg = outpipename      (./outpipe by default)
       3rd arg = size of chunks   ( infinite by default)
     */

    if (argc > 1)
        strcpy (infile, argv[1]);
    if (argc > 2)
        strcpy (outpipe, argv[2]);
    if (argc > 3)
        nbuf = atoi (argv[3]);
```

```
    printf ("Input file: %s,  Output pipe: %s\n", infile, outpipe);
    fflush (NULL);

    if ((fd_in = open (infile, O_RDONLY)) < 0)
        DEATH ("open fd_in");

    if ((fd_out = open (outpipe, O_WRONLY)) < 0)
        DEATH ("open fd_out");

    do {
        if ((rc = splice (fd_in, NULL, fd_out, NULL, nbuf, 0)) < 0)
            DEATH ("splice");
        printf ("Transferred %8d bytes\n", rc);
    } while (rc > 0);

    close (fd_in);
    close (fd_out);

    printf ("done\n");
    exit (EXIT_SUCCESS);
}
```

Chapter 15

Asynchronous I/O

15.1 Lab 1: Testing Asynchronous I/O with POSIX and Linux API's

- Write a program that uses the native **Linux API**. Have it send out a number of write and read requests and synchronize properly. You can work with a disposable file.

- We also present a solution using the **Posix API** for the application.

- Make sure you compile by linking with the right libraries; use -laio for the **Linux API** and -lrt for the **Posix API**. (You can use both in either case as they don't conflict.)

lab1_aio_test.c

```
/* Copyright 2009, J Cooperstein coop@coopj.com (GPLv2) */
#include <stdio.h>
#include <stdlib.h>
#include <unistd.h>
#include <string.h>
#include <fcntl.h>
```

```c
#include <errno.h>
#include <libaio.h>
#include <sys/stat.h>

#define NBYTES 32
#define NBUF   100

void printbufs (char **buf, int nbytes)
{
    int j;
    fflush (stdout);
    for (j = 0; j < NBUF; j++) {
        write (STDOUT_FILENO, buf[j], nbytes);
        printf ("\n");
    }
    printf ("\n");
}

int main (int argc, char *argv[])
{
    int fd, rc, j, k, nbytes = NBYTES, maxevents = NBUF;
    char *buf[NBUF], *filename = "/tmp/testfile";
    struct iocb *iocbray[NBUF], *iocb;
    off_t offset;
    io_context_t ctx = 0;
    struct io_event events[2 * NBUF];
    struct timespec timeout = { 0, 0 };

    /* open or create the file and fill it with a pattern */

    if (argc > 1)
        filename = argv[1];

    printf ("opening %s\n", filename);

    /* notice opening with these flags won't hurt a device node! */

    if ((fd = open (filename, O_RDWR | O_CREAT | O_TRUNC,
                    S_IRUSR | S_IWUSR | S_IRGRP | S_IWGRP)) < 0) {
        printf ("couldn't open %s, ABORTING\n", filename);
        exit (-1);
    }

    /* write initial data out, clear buffers, allocate iocb's */

    for (j = 0; j < NBUF; j++) {
        /* no need to zero iocbs; will be done in io_prep_pread */
        iocbray[j] = malloc (sizeof (struct iocb));
        buf[j] = malloc (nbytes);
        sprintf (buf[j], "%4d%4d%4d%4d%4d%4d%4d%4d", j, j, j, j, j, j, j, j);
        write (fd, buf[j], nbytes);
        memset (buf[j], 0, nbytes);
    }
    printf ("\n");
```

```
/* prepare the context */

rc = io_setup (maxevents, &ctx);
printf (" rc from io_setup = %d\n", rc);

/* (async) read the data from the file */

printf (" reading initial data from the file:\n");

for (j = 0; j < NBUF; j++) {
    iocb = iocbray[j];
    offset = j * nbytes;
    io_prep_pread (iocb, fd, (void *)buf[j], nbytes, offset);
    rc = io_submit (ctx, 1, &iocb);
}

/* sync up and print out the readin data */

while ((rc = io_getevents (ctx, NBUF, NBUF, events, &timeout)) > 0) {
    printf (" rc from io_getevents on the read = %d\n\n", rc);
}

printbufs (buf, nbytes);

/* filling in the buffers before the write */

for (j = 0; j < NBUF; j++) {
    char *tmp = buf[j];
    for (k = 0; k < nbytes; k++) {
        sprintf ((tmp + k), "%1d", j);
    }
}

/* write the changed buffers out */

printf (" writing new data to the file:\n");
for (j = 0; j < NBUF; j++) {
    iocb = iocbray[j];
    offset = j * nbytes;
    io_prep_pwrite (iocb, fd, buf[j], nbytes, offset);
    rc = io_submit (ctx, 1, &iocb);
}

/* sync up again */

while ((rc = io_getevents (ctx, NBUF, NBUF, events, &timeout)) > 0) {
    printf (" rc from io_getevents on the write = %d\n\n", rc);
}

printbufs (buf, nbytes);

/* clean up */
rc = io_destroy (ctx);
close (fd);
exit (0);
```

```
}
```

lab1_posix_test.c

```c
/* Copyright 2009, J Cooperstein coop@coopj.com (GPLv2) */
#include <stdio.h>
#include <stdlib.h>
#include <unistd.h>
#include <string.h>
#include <fcntl.h>
#include <errno.h>
#include <aio.h>
#include <sys/stat.h>

#define NBYTES 32
#define NBUF    100

void printbufs (char **buf, int nbytes)
{
    int j;
    fflush (stdout);
    for (j = 0; j < NBUF; j++) {
        write (STDOUT_FILENO, buf[j], nbytes);
        printf ("\n");
    }
    printf ("\n");
}

int main (int argc, char *argv[])
{
    int fd, rc, j, k, nbytes = NBYTES;
    char *tmp, *buf[NBUF], *filename = "/tmp/testfile";
    struct aiocb *cbray[NBUF], *cb;

    /* create the file and fill it with a pattern */

    if (argc > 1)
        filename = argv[1];

    /* notice opening with these flags won't hurt a device node! */

    if ((fd = open (filename, O_RDWR | O_CREAT | O_TRUNC,
                    S_IRUSR | S_IWUSR | S_IRGRP | S_IWGRP)) < 0) {
        printf ("couldn't open %s, ABORTING\n", filename);
        exit (-1);
    }

    /* write initial data out, clear buffers, allocate aiocb's */

    for (j = 0; j < NBUF; j++) {

        buf[j] = malloc (nbytes);
        sprintf (buf[j], "%4d%4d%4d%4d%4d%4d%4d%4d", j, j, j, j, j, j, j, j);
        write (fd, buf[j], nbytes);
        memset (buf[j], 0, nbytes);
```

```
        cb = malloc (sizeof (struct aiocb));
        cbray[j] = cb;
        memset (cb, 0, sizeof (struct aiocb));

        cb->aio_fildes = fd;
        cb->aio_nbytes = nbytes;
        cb->aio_offset = j * nbytes;
        cb->aio_buf = (void *)buf[j];
    }
    printf ("\n");

    /* (async) read the data from the file */

    printf (" reading initial data from the file:\n");

    for (j = 0; j < NBUF; j++) {
        cb = cbray[j];
        rc = aio_read (cb);
    }

    /* sync up and print out the readin data */

    for (j = 0; j < NBUF; j++) {
        cb = cbray[j];
        while (aio_error (cb) == EINPROGRESS) {
        };
        printf ("%d:  aio_error=%d  aio_return=%d\n  ",
                j, aio_error (cb), (int)aio_return (cb));
    }

    printbufs (buf, nbytes);

    /* filling in the buffers before the write */

    for (j = 0; j < NBUF; j++) {
        tmp = buf[j];
        for (k = 0; k < nbytes; k++) {
            sprintf ((tmp + k), "%1d", j);
        }
        /*        printf ("%d, %s\n", j, buf[j]); */
    }
    printf ("\n");

    /* write the changed buffers out */

    printf (" writing new data to the file:\n");
    for (j = 0; j < NBUF; j++) {
        cb = cbray[j];
        rc = aio_write (cb);
    }

    /* sync up again */

    for (j = 0; j < NBUF; j++) {
```

```
        cb = cbray[j];
        while (aio_error (cb) == EINPROGRESS) {
        };
        printf ("%d:  aio_error=%d  aio_return=%d\n  ",
                j, aio_error (cb), (int)aio_return (cb));
    }

    printbufs (buf, nbytes);

    close (fd);
    exit (0);
}
```

lab1_testloop.sh

```
#!/bin/bash

# 2/2008 J. Cooperstein (coop@coopj.com) License:GPLv2

file="/tmp/testfile" && [ "$1" != "" ] && file=$1
reps=1000            && [ "$2" != "" ] && reps=$2

echo DOING $reps iterations on $file with ../lab1_aio_test:
time ( n=0 ; \
while [ $n -lt $reps ]
  do ./lab1_aio_test $file > /dev/null
  n=$(($n+1))
done )

echo DOING $reps iterations on $file with ../lab1_posix_test:
time ( n=0; \
while [ $n -lt $reps ]
  do ./lab1_posix_test $file > /dev/null
  n=$(($n+1))
done )
```

Chapter 16

Signals - I

16.1   Lab 1: Signals

- Using the `signal()` interface for installing signal handlers, write a simple program to do something pointless in an infinite loop. (Like printing out the same message after every second.)

- Upon getting a CTRL-C (`SIGINT`) the program should print a message, but not die.

- Upon getting a CTRL-\ (`SIGQUIT`) it should call `abort()` to dump core.

- **Note:** Some **Linux** distributions set the maximum core dump size to 0. Type `ulimit -c` to find out what you actually have. If the maximum core dump size has to be set, do it with `ulimit -c {nbytes}`.

lab1_signal.c

```
/* Copyright 2009, J Cooperstein coop@coopj.com (GPLv2) */

#include <stdio.h>
#include <unistd.h>
#include <signal.h>
```

```
#include <stdlib.h>

/* our signal handlers */

void sig_int (int what)
{
    printf ("We have received SIGINT: Continuing Anyway, Boss.\n");
}
void sig_quit (int what)
{
    printf ("We have received SIGQUIT: Aborting.\n");
    abort ();
}

int main (int argc, char *argv[])
{
    /* Install signal handlers */
    signal (SIGINT, sig_int);   /* for CTRL-C */
    signal (SIGQUIT, sig_quit); /* for CTRL-\ */

    /* Do something pointless, forever */
    for (;;) {
        printf ("This is a pointless message.\n");
        sleep (1);
    }
    exit (0);
}
```

16.2   Lab 2: sigaction()

- Adapt the previous exercise (or start fresh) to use the sigaction() interface. Set up a signal set and mask to do this.

- Have the SIGINT handler sleep for a couple of seconds; what happens if you send a SIGQUIT while it is sleeping?

lab2_sigaction.c

```
 /* Copyright 2009, J Cooperstein coop@coopj.com (GPLv2) */

#include <stdio.h>
#include <unistd.h>
#include <signal.h>
#include <stdlib.h>
#include <errno.h>
#include <string.h>

#define DEATH(mess) { perror(mess); exit(errno); }

/* our signal handlers */

void sig_int (int what)
```

```
{
    printf ("We have received SIGINT: Will sleep for 2 seconds and continue\n");
    sleep (2);
    printf (" done sleeping 2 seconds\n");
}

void sig_quit (int what)
{
    printf ("We have received SIGQUIT: Aborting.\n");
    abort ();
}

int main (int argc, char *argv[])
{
    struct sigaction act;

    memset (&act, 0, sizeof (act));

    /* Install signal handlers */
    act.sa_handler = sig_int;
    if (sigaction (SIGINT, &act, NULL) < 0) /* for CTRL-C */
        DEATH ("sigaction");

    printf ("Successfully installed signal handler for SIGINT\n");

    act.sa_handler = sig_quit;
    if (sigaction (SIGQUIT, &act, NULL) < 0)    /* for CTRL-\ */
        DEATH ("sigaction");

    printf ("Successfully installed signal handler for SIGQUIT\n");

    /* Do something pointless, forever */
    for (;;) {
        printf ("This is a pointless message.\n");
        sleep (1);
    }

    exit (0);
}
```

16.3   Lab 3: Blocking Signals

* Adapt the previous exercise so that SIGQUIT is blocked while the handler for SIGINT is running.

lab3_block.c

```
/* Copyright 2009, J Cooperstein coop@coopj.com (GPLv2) */

#include <stdio.h>
#include <unistd.h>
#include <signal.h>
#include <stdlib.h>
```

```
#include <errno.h>
#include <string.h>

#define DEATH(mess) { perror(mess); exit(errno); }

/* our signal handlers */
void sig_int (int what)
{
    printf ("We have received SIGINT:"
            "Will sleep for 5  seconds and continue\n");
    sleep (5);
    printf (" done sleeping\n");
}

void sig_quit (int what)
{
    printf ("We have received SIGQUIT: Aborting.\n");
    abort ();
}

int main (int argc, char *argv[])
{
    int rc;
    struct sigaction act_quit, act_int;
    sigset_t sigmask;

    memset (&act_quit, 0, sizeof (act_quit));
    memset (&act_int, 0, sizeof (act_int));

    /* set up signal mask to block SIGQUIT during SIGINT */

    rc = sigemptyset (&sigmask);
    printf ("rc = %d from sigemptyset\n", rc);
    rc = sigaddset (&sigmask, SIGQUIT);
    printf ("rc = %d from sigaddset\n", rc);

    /* Install signal handlers */
    act_int.sa_handler = sig_int;
    act_int.sa_mask = sigmask;

    if (sigaction (SIGINT, &act_int, NULL) < 0) /* for CTRL-C */
        DEATH ("sigaction");
    printf ("Successfully installed signal handler for SIGINT\n");

    act_quit.sa_handler = sig_quit;
    if (sigaction (SIGQUIT, &act_quit, NULL) < 0)   /* for CTRL-\ */
        DEATH ("sigaction");

    printf ("Successfully installed signal handler for SIGQUIT\n");

    /* Do something pointless, forever */
    for (;;) {
        printf ("This is a pointless message.\n");
        sleep (1);
    }
```

```
    exit (0);
}
```

16.4   Lab 4: Examining Signal Priorities.

- In the below, do not send or handle either of the signals `SIGKILL` or `SIGSTOP`.

- Write a **C** program that includes a signal handler that can handle any signal. The handler should avoid making any system calls (such as those that might occur doing I/O).

- The handler should simply store the sequence of signals as they come in, and update a counter array for each signal that indicates how many times the signal has been handled.

- The program should begin by suspending processing of all signals (using `sigprocmask()`.

- It should then install the new set of signal handlers (which can be the same for all signals, registering them with the `sigaction()` interface.

- The program should send every possible signal to itself multiple times, using the `raise()` function.

- Signal processing should be resumed, once again using `sigprocmask()`.

- Before completing, the program should print out statistics including:

  - The total number of times each signal was received.
  - The order in which the signals were received, noting each time the total number of times that signal had been received up to that point.

- Note the following items:

  - If more than one of a given signal is raised while the process has blocked it, does the process receive it multiple times?
  - Are all signals received by the process, or are some handled before they reach it?
  - What order are the signals received in?

- One signal, `SIGCONT` (18 on **x86**) may not get through; can you figure out why?

- It appears that in the 2.6 kernel signals 32 and 33 can not be blocked and will cause your program to fail. Even though header files indicate `SIGRTMIN=32`, the command `kill -l` indicates `SIGRTMIN=34`.

- Note that one should always be using signal names, not numbers, which are allowed to be completely implementation dependent.

- Avoid sending these signals.

---

lab4_sigorder.c

```
/* Copyright 2009, J Cooperstein coop@coopj.com (GPLv2) */

#include <stdio.h>
#include <unistd.h>
#include <signal.h>
#include <stdlib.h>
#include <string.h>
#include <pthread.h>

#define NUMSIGS 64

/* prototypes of locally-defined signal handlers */

void (sig_handler) (int);

int sig_count[NUMSIGS + 1];        /* counter for signals received */
volatile static int line = 0;
volatile int signumbuf[6400], sigcountbuf[6400];

int main (int argc, char *argv[])
{
    sigset_t sigmask_new, sigmask_old;
    struct sigaction sigact, oldact;
    int signum, rc, i;
    pid_t pid;

    pid = getpid ();

    /* block all possible signals */
    rc = sigfillset (&sigmask_new);
    rc = sigprocmask (SIG_SETMASK, &sigmask_new, &sigmask_old);

    /* Assign values to members of sigaction structures */
    memset (&sigact, 0, sizeof (struct sigaction));
    sigact.sa_handler = sig_handler;      /* we use a pointer to a handler */
    sigact.sa_flags = 0;          /* no flags */
    /* VERY IMPORTANT */
    sigact.sa_mask = sigmask_new;    /* block signals in the handler itself  */

    /*
     * Now, use sigaction to create references to local signal
     * handlers * and raise the signal to myself
     */

    printf
        ("\nInstalling signal handler and Raising signal for signal number:\n\n");
    for (signum = 1; signum <= NUMSIGS; signum++) {
        if (signum == SIGKILL || signum == SIGSTOP || signum == 32
            || signum == 33) {
            printf ("  --");
            continue;
        }
        sigaction (signum, &sigact, &oldact);
```

```
        /* send the signal 3 times! */
        rc = raise (signum);
        rc = raise (signum);
        rc = raise (signum);
        if (rc) {
            printf ("Failed on Signal %d\n", signum);
        } else {
            printf ("%4d", signum);
            if (signum % 16 == 0)
                printf ("\n");
        }
    }
    fflush (stdout);

    /* restore original mask */
    rc = sigprocmask (SIG_SETMASK, &sigmask_old, NULL);

    printf ("\nSignal  Number(Times Processed)\n");
    printf ("-----------------------------------------------\n");
    for (i = 1; i <= NUMSIGS; i++) {
        printf ("%4d:%3d  ", i, sig_count[i]);
        if (i % 8 == 0)
            printf ("\n");
    }
    printf ("\n");

    printf ("\nHistory: Signal  Number(Count Processed)\n");
    printf ("-----------------------------------------------\n");
    for (i = 0; i < line; i++) {
        if (i % 8 == 0)
            printf ("\n");
        printf ("%4d(%1d)", signumbuf[i], sigcountbuf[i]);
    }
    printf ("\n");
    exit (0);
}

void sig_handler (int sig)
{
    sig_count[sig]++;
    signumbuf[line] = sig;
    sigcountbuf[line] = sig_count[sig];
    line++;
}
```

Chapter 17

Signals - II

17.1 Lab 1: Using siginfo and sigqueue().

- Take the simple example using `sigqueue()` and expand it to pass a structure into the enhanced signal handler.

- Do this a number of times and print out values of interest.

lab1_siginfo.c

```
/* Copyright 2009, J Cooperstein coop@coopj.com (GPLv2) */

#include <stdio.h>
#include <unistd.h>
#include <signal.h>
#include <stdlib.h>
#include <errno.h>
#include <string.h>

#define DEATH(mess) { perror(mess); exit(errno); }
```

```
struct my_s
{
    int x;
    char s[32];
};

/* our signal handlers */

void sig_act (int sig, siginfo_t * si, void *a)
{
    struct my_s *s = si->si_ptr;
    printf ("in handler pid=%d, SIGNAL = %d\n", getpid (), sig);

    printf ("si_signo = \t%d\n", si->si_signo);
    printf ("si_code = \t%d\n", si->si_code);
    printf ("si_pid = \t%d\n", si->si_pid);
    printf ("si_uid = \t%d\n", si->si_uid);
    printf ("si_ptr.x = \t%d\n", s->x);
    printf ("si_ptr.s = \t%s\n", s->s);
}

int main (int argc, char *argv[])
{
    struct sigaction act;
    struct my_s s;
    int j, sig = SIGINT;
    union sigval sv;

    if (argc > 1)
        sig = atoi (argv[1]);

    memset (&act, 0, sizeof (act));
    act.sa_sigaction = sig_act;
    act.sa_flags = SA_SIGINFO;
    if (sigaction (sig, &act, NULL) < 0)     /* for CTRL-C */
        DEATH ("sigaction");

    printf ("pid=%d Successfully installed signal handler for signal=%d\n",
            getpid (), sig);

    for (j = 0; j < 3; j++) {
        printf ("This is a pointless message\n");
        s.x = j * 100;
        strcpy (s.s, "hello buddy");
        sv.sival_ptr = &s;
        printf ("sigqueue returns %d\n", sigqueue (getpid (), sig, sv));
        sleep (1);
    }
    exit (0);
}
```

17.2 Lab 2: Using sigsetjmp() and siglongjmp().

- Write a simple program with a signal handler for SIGINT (Control-C). Have the signal handler return with a call to siglongjmp() to a point in your main program where sigsetjmp() is invoked.

- For the first four times the signal handler is hit have the program continue; the fifth time have it terminate.

lab2_siglongjmp.c

```
/* Copyright 2009, J Cooperstein coop@coopj.com (GPLv2) */

#include <stdio.h>
#include <unistd.h>
#include <signal.h>
#include <stdlib.h>
#include <errno.h>
#include <string.h>
#include <setjmp.h>

#define DEATH(mess) { perror(mess); exit(errno); }

sigjmp_buf env;
int savesigs = 1;

/* our signal handlers */

void sig_int (int what)
{
    static int val = 0;
    val++;
    printf ("We have received SIGINT: val = %d\n", val);
    siglongjmp (env, val);
}

int main (int argc, char *argv[])
{
    int rc;
    struct sigaction act;
    memset (&act, 0, sizeof (act));

    /* Install signal handlers */
    act.sa_handler = sig_int;
    if (sigaction (SIGINT, &act, NULL) < 0) /* for CTRL-C */
        DEATH ("sigaction");

    printf ("Successfully installed signal handler for SIGINT\n");

    rc = sigsetjmp (env, savesigs);
    printf ("rc from sigsetmp = %d\n", rc);

    if (rc == 4) {
        printf ("I'm returning non-locally and then I'm going to quit\n");
```

```
        exit (EXIT_SUCCESS);
    }

    for (;;) {
        printf ("Going to wait for a signal with pause()\n");
        pause ();
        printf ("I rejoined inside the sleep loop\n");
    }
    /* should never reach here */
    exit (EXIT_FAILURE);
}
```

Chapter 18

POSIX Threads - I

18.1   Lab 1: Threads

- Write a counting program, which should have two threads.

- While one thread loops, incrementing a counter as fast as it can, the other one occasionally peeks at the counter and prints out its value.

lab1_counter.c

```
/* Copyright 2009, J Cooperstein coop@coopj.com (GPLv2) */

#include <stdio.h>
#include <stdlib.h>
#include <pthread.h>
#include <unistd.h>
#include <errno.h>

#define DEATH(mess) { perror(mess); exit(errno); }

volatile char running = 1;
```

```
volatile static long long counter = 0;   /* if not volatile, won't work when
                                             optimization is turned on */


/* This is the "computational" thread */
void *process (void *arg)
{
    while (running) {
        counter++;
    };
    pthread_exit (NULL);
}


/* This is the "user interface" thread */
int main (int argc, char **argv)
{
    int i;
    pthread_t threadId;
    void *retval;

    /* Start up the processing thread. */
    if (pthread_create (&threadId, NULL, process, "0"))
        DEATH ("pthread_create");

    /* Every so often, look at the counter and print it out. */
    for (i = 0; i < 10; i++) {
        sleep (1);
        printf ("%lld\n", counter);
    }

    /* Tell the processing thread to quit. */
    running = 0;

    /* Wait for the processing thread to quit. */
    if (pthread_join (threadId, &retval))
        DEATH ("pthread_join");

    return 0;
}
```

18.2   Lab 2: Signals and Threads

- Write a program that launches multiple threads, which has one thread reserved for dealing with signals, using `sigwait()`, `pthread_sigmask()`.

- Send one or more signals to the process either from the command line (you can use `SIGINT` which is `Control-C`), or using `kill()`.

- Verify which thread deals with the signals using `pthread_self()` to print out the thread ID's.

lab2_signal.c

```
/* Copyright 2009, J Cooperstein coop@coopj.com (GPLv2) */
```

```c
#include <unistd.h>
#include <stdlib.h>
#include <stdio.h>
#include <pthread.h>
#include <signal.h>

#define NUM_THREADS 10

void *sigfun (void *arg)
{
    int sigreceived;

    sigset_t sigmask;
    sigfillset (&sigmask);
    printf (" Signal Handling Thread %ld starting\n", pthread_self ());
    while (1) {
        sigwait (&sigmask, &sigreceived);
        printf (" Signal Handling Thread %ld received signal %d\n",
                pthread_self (), sigreceived);
    }
    printf (" Signal Handling Thread %ld exiting\n", pthread_self ());
    pthread_exit (NULL);
}

void *fun (void *arg)
{
    printf ("              Thread %ld starting\n", pthread_self ());
    pause ();                    /* will return when any signal is received */
    printf ("              Thread %ld exiting\n", pthread_self ());
    pthread_exit (NULL);
}

int main (int argc, char *argv[])
{
    int i;

    pthread_t threads[NUM_THREADS];
    sigset_t sigmask;

    sigemptyset (&sigmask);
    sigaddset (&sigmask, SIGINT);
    pthread_sigmask (SIG_BLOCK, &sigmask, NULL);

    printf ("Master thread id = %ld\n", (long)pthread_self ());

    pthread_create (&threads[0], NULL, sigfun, NULL);
    printf ("I created signal handling thread id=%ld\n", (long)threads[0]);

    for (i = 1; i < NUM_THREADS; i++) {
        pthread_create (&threads[i], NULL, fun, NULL);
        printf ("I created thread id=%ld\n", (long)threads[i]);
    }

    sleep (1);
    printf ("Sending SIGINT (Ctl-C)\n");
```

```
    kill (getpid (), SIGINT);

    sleep (3);

    exit (0);

}
```

18.3   Lab 3: Signals, Threads and Handlers

- Instead of dedicating one thread to signals, install a signal handler.

- After launching a number of threads, block handling the signal in the master thread.

- Send one or more signals to the process either from the command line (you can use `SIGINT` which is `Control-C`), or using `kill()`.

- Verify which thread deals with the signals using `pthread_self()` to print out the thread ID's.

lab3_sighandler.c

```c
/* Copyright 2009, J Cooperstein coop@coopj.com (GPLv2) */

#include <unistd.h>
#include <stdlib.h>
#include <stdio.h>
#include <pthread.h>
#include <signal.h>

#define NUM_THREADS 10

void sighand (int sig)
{
    printf ("Im executing signal handler in thread %ld\n", pthread_self ());
}

void *tfun (void *arg)
{
    printf ("            Thread %ld starting\n", pthread_self ());
    pause ();                    /* will return when any signal is received */
    printf ("            Thread %ld exiting\n", pthread_self ());
    pthread_exit (NULL);
}

int main (int argc, char *argv[])
{
    int i;

    pthread_t threads[NUM_THREADS];
    sigset_t sigmask;
    struct sigaction act;
```

```
    act.sa_handler = sighand;
    if (sigaction (SIGINT, &act, NULL) < 0) {
        printf ("Failed to install signal handler\n");
        exit (-1);
    }

    printf ("Master thread id = %ld\n", (long)pthread_self ());

    for (i = 0; i < NUM_THREADS; i++) {
        pthread_create (&threads[i], NULL, tfun, NULL);
        printf ("I created thread id=%ld\n", (long)threads[i]);
    }

    /* block the signal in the master thread  only */

    sigemptyset (&sigmask);
    sigaddset (&sigmask, SIGINT);
    pthread_sigmask (SIG_BLOCK, &sigmask, NULL);

    /* for fun send the signals to myself
       disable this to send Ctl-C from command line */

    for (i = 0; i < NUM_THREADS; i++) {
        kill (getpid (), SIGINT);
        sched_yield ();             /* Could also do a  sleep(1); */
    }

    /* wait for the threads to terminate */

    for (i = 0; i < NUM_THREADS; i++) {
        pthread_join (threads[i], NULL);
        printf ("Master thread joined with thread %d\n", i);
    }

    exit (0);

}
```

18.4   Lab 4: Threads and Initialization and Exit Handlers

- Extend the counter exercise to have constructor and destructor functions.

- Are they run for each thread? Or for only the master thread?

lab4_constdest.c

```
/* Copyright 2009, J Cooperstein coop@coopj.com (GPLv2) */

#include <stdio.h>
#include <stdlib.h>
#include <pthread.h>
#include <unistd.h>
#include <errno.h>
```

```
void init_fun (void) __attribute__ ((constructor));
void exit_fun (void) __attribute__ ((destructor));

void init_fun (void)
{
    printf ("I am in init_fun\n");
}
void exit_fun (void)
{
    printf ("I am in exit_fun\n");
}


#define DEATH(mess) { perror(mess); exit(errno); }

volatile char running = 1;
volatile static long long counter = 0;   /* if not volatile, won't work when
                                            optimization is turned on */


/* This is the "computational" thread */
void *process (void *arg)
{
    while (running) {
        counter++;
    };
    pthread_exit (NULL);
}

/* This is the "user interface" thread */
int main (int argc, char **argv)
{
    int i;
    pthread_t threadId;
    void *retval;

    /* Start up the processing thread. */
    if (pthread_create (&threadId, NULL, process, "0"))
        DEATH ("pthread_create");

    /* Every so often, look at the counter and print it out. */
    for (i = 0; i < 10; i++) {
        sleep (1);
        printf ("%lld\n", counter);
    }

    /* Tell the processing thread to quit. */
    running = 0;

    /* Wait for the processing thread to quit. */
    if (pthread_join (threadId, &retval))
        DEATH ("pthread_join");

    return 0;
}
```

Chapter 19

POSIX Threads - II

19.1   Lab 1: Threads with Mutexes

- Extend the counter exercise from the previous section previous exercise to protect the counter variable with a mutex.

- What happens if the counter thread exits while holding the mutex? Does it release the lock?

lab1_mutex.c

```c
/* Copyright 2009, J Cooperstein coop@coopj.com (GPLv2) */

#include <stdio.h>
#include <stdlib.h>
#include <pthread.h>
#include <unistd.h>
#include <errno.h>

#define DEATH(mess) { perror(mess); exit(errno); }

static char running = 1;          /* note this can be static now! */
```

```
static long long counter = 0;

pthread_mutex_t c_mutex;

/* This is the "computational" thread */
void *process (void *arg)
{
    while (running) {
        pthread_mutex_lock (&c_mutex);
        counter++;
        pthread_mutex_unlock (&c_mutex);
    }
    pthread_exit (NULL);
}

/* This is the "user interface" thread */
int main (int argc, char **argv)
{
    int i;
    pthread_t threadId;
    void *retval;

    /* Initialize a mutex with default attributes */
    pthread_mutex_init (&c_mutex, NULL);

    /* Start up the processing thread. */
    if (pthread_create (&threadId, NULL, process, "0"))
        DEATH ("pthread_create");

    /* Every so often, look at the counter and print it out. */
    for (i = 0; i < 10; i++) {
        sleep (1);
        pthread_mutex_lock (&c_mutex);
        printf ("%lld\n", counter);
        pthread_mutex_unlock (&c_mutex);
    }

    /* Tell the processing thread to quit. */
    running = 0;

    /* Wait for the processing thread to quit. */
    if (pthread_join (threadId, &retval))
        DEATH ("pthread_join");

    return 0;
}
```

lab1_mutex_exitwithlock.c

```
/* Copyright 2009, J Cooperstein coop@coopj.com (GPLv2) */

#include <stdio.h>
#include <stdlib.h>
#include <pthread.h>
#include <unistd.h>
```

```
#include <errno.h>

#define DEATH(mess) { perror(mess); exit(errno); }

static char running = 1;          /* note this can be static now! */
static long long counter = 0;

pthread_mutex_t c_mutex;
int i;

/* This is the "computational" thread */
void *process (void *arg)
{
    while (running) {
        pthread_mutex_lock (&c_mutex);
        if (i > 4)
            pthread_exit (NULL);
        counter++;
        pthread_mutex_unlock (&c_mutex);
    }
    pthread_exit (NULL);
}


/* This is the "user interface" thread */
int main (int argc, char **argv)
{
    pthread_t threadId;
    void *retval;

    /* Initialize a mutex with default attributes */
    pthread_mutex_init (&c_mutex, NULL);

    /* Start up the processing thread. */
    if (pthread_create (&threadId, NULL, process, "0"))
        DEATH ("pthread_create");

    /* Every so often, look at the counter and print it out. */
    for (i = 0; i < 10; i++) {
        sleep (1);
        pthread_mutex_lock (&c_mutex);
        printf ("%lld\n", counter);
        pthread_mutex_unlock (&c_mutex);
    }

    /* Tell the processing thread to quit. */
    running = 0;

    /* Wait for the processing thread to quit. */
    if (pthread_join (threadId, &retval))
        DEATH ("pthread_join");

    return 0;
}
```

19.2   Lab 2: POSIX Semaphores and Threads

- Modify the **pthreads** exercise (which may have already been enhanced to use **mutexes**), to use POSIX semaphores to protect the counter variable.

lab2_sem.c

```
/* Copyright 2009, J Cooperstein coop@coopj.com (GPLv2) */

#include <stdio.h>
#include <stdlib.h>
#include <pthread.h>
#include <unistd.h>
#include <errno.h>

#include <semaphore.h>

#define DEATH(mess) { perror(mess); exit(errno); }

/* volatile char running = 1; */
static char running = 1;          /* note this can be static now! */
static long long counter = 0;

sem_t c_sem;

/* This is the "computational" thread */
void *process (void *arg)
{
    while (running) {
        sem_wait (&c_sem);
        counter++;
        sem_post (&c_sem);
    }
    pthread_exit (NULL);
}

/* This is the "user interface" thread */
int main (int argc, char **argv)
{
    int i;
    pthread_t threadId;
    void *retval;

    /* Initialize a semaphore up */
    sem_init (&c_sem, 0, 1);

    /* Start up the processing thread. */
    if (pthread_create (&threadId, NULL, process, "0"))
        DEATH ("pthread_create");

    /* Every so often, look at the counter and print it out. */
    for (i = 0; i < 10; i++) {
        sleep (1);
        sem_wait (&c_sem);
```

```
        printf ("%lld\n", counter);
        sem_post (&c_sem);
    }

    /* Tell the processing thread to quit. */
    running = 0;

    /* Wait for the processing thread to quit. */
    if (pthread_join (threadId, &retval))
        DEATH ("pthread_join");

    return 0;
}
```

19.3   Lab 3: Condition Variables

- Write a program that creates four threads and a counter.

- Have one thread wait for input, with `scanf("%d", &val)`. After getting the value it should (safely) add that value to the counter.

- Meanwhile, the other three threads should be be in a loop. In each loop, they should:

  - Wait for the counter to be greater than zero.
  - Decrement the counter; print a message with their thread ID (get it from `pthread_self()`) and the counter value.
  - Sleep for one second.

- You should hold a lock when looking at or changing the counter, but not at any other time - especially not when sleeping or waiting for user input!

- If you want to be really good, try not even holding the lock when you are printing. Make sure that you don't refer to the counter outside of the lock though.

lab3_cond.c

```
/* Copyright 2009, J Cooperstein coop@coopj.com (GPLv2) */

#include <unistd.h>
#include <stdlib.h>
#include <stdio.h>
#include <pthread.h>

#define NUM_WORKERS 3

static pthread_mutex_t lock = PTHREAD_MUTEX_INITIALIZER;
static pthread_cond_t cond = PTHREAD_COND_INITIALIZER;

/*
 * Both the counter and the "exiting" flag are protected by the lock.
 */
static volatile int counter = 0;
```

```
static volatile int exiting = 0;

/*
 * Wait for some data to show up in the counter. Then "process" the data.
 * To process the data I just decrement the counter and sleep for a second.
 *
 * Parameters:
 *    arg - Not used.
 * Return value:
 *    Not used; always returns NULL.
 */
void *decrementer (void *arg)
{
    int counterVal;

    for (;;) {
        /*
         * Lock the mutex so we can safely examine the counter and the
         * "exiting" flag.
         */
        pthread_mutex_lock (&lock);
        while (!exiting && (counter <= 0)) {
            /*
             * "cond" should be signalled when the counter
             * is incremented or the "exiting" flag is set, so we will wake up as
             * soon as we have something to do.
             */
            pthread_cond_wait (&cond, &lock);
        }
        if (exiting) {
            pthread_mutex_unlock (&lock);
            pthread_exit (NULL);
        }
        /*
         * We copy "counter" into the local "counterVal" so that we can print it
         * out after releasing the lock.
         */
        counterVal = --counter;
        pthread_mutex_unlock (&lock);

        printf ("Thread %ld decrementing to %d.\n",
                pthread_self (), counterVal);
        sleep (1);
    }
}

int main (int argc, char *argv[])
{
    pthread_t threads[NUM_WORKERS];
    int i, val;

    for (i = 0; i < NUM_WORKERS; ++i) {
        pthread_create (&threads[i], NULL, decrementer, NULL);
    }
    for (;;) {
```

```
    switch (scanf ("%d", &val)) {
    case 1:
        /*
         * We got a value to add to the counter. Add it, then broadcast to
         * cond to wake up any threads waiting for something to do.
         */
        pthread_mutex_lock (&lock);
        counter += val;
        pthread_cond_broadcast (&cond);
        pthread_mutex_unlock (&lock);
        break;

    case EOF:
        /*
         * We got an EOF, so we set the "exiting" flag, broadcast to the workers,
         * then wait for them all to exit cleanly before we close up the
         * application.
         */
        pthread_mutex_lock (&lock);
        exiting = 1;
        pthread_cond_broadcast (&cond);
        pthread_mutex_unlock (&lock);
        for (i = 0; i < NUM_WORKERS; ++i) {
            pthread_join (threads[i], NULL);
        }
        exit (0);

    default:
        fprintf (stderr,
                "You must enter numbers or EOF to end the program.\n");
        exit (1);
    }
  }
}
```

19.4   Lab 4: Producer/Consumer

- Write a multi-threaded program that has one or more producers and one or more consumers, each producer and consumer being represented by a thread.

- The producers create a data event, which can be as simple as storing an index in a structure, while the consumers use the event.

- There should be a maximum number of events that can be buffered by producers before consumers eliminate them.

- The solution is implemented in terms of condition variables; you can probably can find other methods, such as using semaphores.

lab4_prodcons.c

```
/* Copyright 2009, J Cooperstein coop@coopj.com (GPLv2) */
#include <unistd.h>
```

```c
#include <stdlib.h>
#include <stdio.h>
#include <pthread.h>

#define NMAX 200
#define NBUF 24
#define NPROD 4
#define NCONS 7

static pthread_cond_t cond_not_empty = PTHREAD_COND_INITIALIZER;
static pthread_cond_t cond_not_full = PTHREAD_COND_INITIALIZER;
static pthread_mutex_t lock = PTHREAD_MUTEX_INITIALIZER;

int j_produced = 0, j_consumed = 0, nbuf = NBUF, nmax = NMAX;
volatile int j_active = 0;

struct event
{
    int location;
};

struct event **buf_struct;

void produce (int j)
{                                  /* j runs from 1 to nbuf */
    int location = (j - 1) % nbuf;
    buf_struct[location]->location = location;
    printf ("          PRODUCE: loc = %3d, id=%3d\n", location,
            (int)pthread_self () % 1000);
}

void consume (int j)
{                                  /* j runs from 1 to nbuf */
    int location = (j - 1) % nbuf;
    buf_struct[location]->location = location;
    printf ("          CONSUME: loc = %3d, id=%3d\n", location,
            (int)pthread_self () % 1000);
}

#define PRO_QUIT { \
        printf ("Exiting the producer thread, id=%3d\n", (int)pthread_self()%1000); \
        pthread_exit (0); }
#define PRO_CHECK { \
    if ( j_produced == nmax){ pthread_mutex_unlock(&lock); PRO_QUIT; }}

void *producer (void *arg)
{
    printf ("Starting the producer thread, id=%3d\n",
            (int)pthread_self () % 1000);
    while (j_produced < nmax) {
        pthread_mutex_lock (&lock);
        while (j_active >= nbuf) {
            PRO_CHECK;
            pthread_cond_wait (&cond_not_full, &lock);
        }
```

```
                PRO_CHECK;
                j_produced++;
                j_active++;
                printf ("prod %3d, active %3d, id=%3d", j_produced, j_active,
                        (int)pthread_self () % 1000);
                produce (j_produced);
                pthread_cond_broadcast (&cond_not_empty);
                pthread_mutex_unlock (&lock);
        }
        PRO_QUIT;

}


#define CON_QUIT { \
        printf ("Exiting the consumer thread, id=%3d\n", (int)pthread_self()%1000); \
        pthread_exit (0); }
#define CON_CHECK { \
    if ( j_consumed == nmax ) { pthread_mutex_unlock (&lock); CON_QUIT; } }

void *consumer (void *arg)
{
    printf ("Starting the consumer thread, id=%3d\n",
            (int)pthread_self () % 1000);
    while (j_consumed < nmax) {
        pthread_mutex_lock (&lock);
        while (j_active == 0) {
            CON_CHECK;
            pthread_cond_wait (&cond_not_empty, &lock);
        }
        CON_CHECK;
        j_consumed++;
        printf ("cons %3d, active %3d, id=%3d", j_consumed, j_active,
                (int)pthread_self () % 1000);
        consume (j_consumed);
        j_active--;
        pthread_cond_broadcast (&cond_not_full);
        pthread_mutex_unlock (&lock);
    }
    CON_QUIT;
}

int main (int argc, char *argv[])
{
    pthread_t t_p[NPROD], t_c[NCONS];
    void *rc;
    int j;
    if (argc > 2) {
        nmax = atoi (argv[1]);
        nbuf = atoi (argv[2]);
    }

    buf_struct = malloc (nbuf * sizeof (unsigned long));

    for (j = 0; j < nbuf; j++)
        buf_struct[j] = malloc (sizeof (struct event));
```

```
    for (j = 0; j < NPROD; j++)
        pthread_create (&t_p[j], NULL, producer, NULL);
    for (j = 0; j < NCONS; j++)
        pthread_create (&t_c[j], NULL, consumer, NULL);

    for (j = 0; j < NPROD; j++)
        pthread_join (t_p[j], &rc);
    for (j = 0; j < NCONS; j++)
        pthread_join (t_c[j], &rc);

    exit (0);
}
```

Chapter 20

Networking and Sockets

20.1   Lab 1: Using netstat to Examine Connections.

- The command line utility **netstat** is an all-purpose tool for examining the state of the various sockets and interfaces active on the system and can be used for other purposes as well, such as examining routing. Typing `netstat -h` will give a brief summary of possiblities.

- Typing `netstat -ae` will give a quick summary of all the information. Typing `netstat -i` will give a summary by interface:

```
$ netstat -i
Kernel Interface table
Iface       MTU Met   RX-OK RX-ERR RX-DRP RX-OVR    TX-OK TX-ERR TX-DRP TX-OVR Flg
eth0       1500   0   98577      0      0      0    83195      0      0      0 BMRU
eth1       1500   0   11560      0      0      0    13574      0      0      0 BMRU
lo        16436   0     106      0      0      0      106      0      0      0 LRU
```

Note that typing `netstat -ie` will give the same output as `ifconfig`.

- Typing

```
$ netstat  -ae --raw --tcp --udp
```

will show information about the state of **raw,   TCP**, and **UDP** sockets.

- To obtain information about **Unix domain sockets**:

```
$ netstat  -ae --unix
```

and to gain global statistics:

```
$ netstat  -as
```

Chapter 21

Sockets - Addresses and Hosts

21.1   Lab 1: Examining Internet Addresses

- Write a program that takes as an argument an Internet address in dot-quad notation, e.g., 127.0.0.1 or 192.168.1.100.

- The program should convert this to a binary address with `inet_aton()` and print out the result.

- The program should convert this to a binary address with `inet_addr()` and print out the result.

- The program should invert the result of `inet_aton()` with `inet_ntoa()` and make sure the original input comes back.

lab1_address.c

```
/* Copyright 2009, J Cooperstein coop@coopj.com (GPLv2) */

#include <stdio.h>
#include <stdlib.h>
#include <sys/socket.h>
#include <netinet/in.h>
```

```c
#include <arpa/inet.h>

int main (int argc, char *argv[])
{
    int rc;
    char *here;
    struct in_addr addr;
    in_addr_t addrb;

    if (argc < 2) {
        printf ("\nUSAGE: %s IP address, try again!\n", argv[0]);
        exit (EXIT_FAILURE);
    }

    here = argv[1];
    printf ("\nThe original address is:            %s\n", here);

    if (!(rc = inet_aton (here, &addr))) {
        printf (" inet_aton failed!\n");
        exit (EXIT_FAILURE);
    }
    printf ("\nFrom inet_aton: %x\n", addr.s_addr);

    addrb = inet_addr (here);
    printf ("From inet_addr: %x\n", addrb);

    printf ("\nThe return address from inet_nota is: %s\n", inet_ntoa (addr));

    exit (EXIT_SUCCESS);
}
```

21.2   Lab 2: Examining Host Entries

- Write a program that takes as input an Internet address and returns information about its address, obtained with `gethostbyname()`.

- Some good examples to try would be:

  ```
  www.us.kernel.org
  localhost
  www.yahoo.com
  google.com
  coopj.com
  ```

- For the address the program should print out:

  – The address name, type, and length.
  – Any aliases.
  – The full list of addresses used by the host.

  i.e., you should dump out the `hostent` structure.

- For a little bit extra, print out the addresses in dotted quad notation, **without** using the helper functions.

- Do all hosts fill in the `aliases` array?

- Compare your results with what you get from typing:

  host <address>

lab2_gethost.c

```c
/* Copyright 2009, J Cooperstein coop@coopj.com (GPLv2) */

#include <stdio.h>
#include <stdlib.h>
#include <string.h>
#include <errno.h>
#include <sys/socket.h>
#include <netinet/in.h>
#include <arpa/inet.h>
#include <netdb.h>

void print_quad (unsigned int x);

int main (int argc, char *argv[])
{
    struct hostent *hent;
    int j;
    struct in_addr addrh;
    char **tmp;

    if (argc < 2) {
        printf ("\nUSAGE: %s address, try again!\n", argv[0]);
        exit (EXIT_FAILURE);
    }

    printf ("\nGetting information on: %s\n", argv[1]);

    if (!(hent = gethostbyname (argv[1]))) {
        herror ("Failed to get the host name");
        exit (EXIT_FAILURE);
    }

    printf ("\nh_name       = %s\n", hent->h_name);
    printf ("h_addrtype   = %d\n", hent->h_addrtype);
    printf ("h_length     = %d\n\n", hent->h_length);

    if (*hent->h_aliases)
        for (j = 0, tmp = hent->h_aliases; *tmp != NULL; j++, tmp++)
            printf ("h_aliases[%d]  = %s\n", j, *tmp);
    else
        printf ("h_aliases[%d]  = %s\n", 0, "No aliases found!");

    printf ("\n");
    for (j = 0; hent->h_addr_list[j] != NULL; j++) {
        memcpy (&addrh, hent->h_addr_list[j], hent->h_length);
        printf ("h_addr_list[%d] = ", j);
        print_quad (addrh.s_addr);
```

```
    }
    printf ("\n");
    exit (EXIT_SUCCESS);
}


/*
   Print out 32 bit network address (in network order) as dotted quad
   note we are going to do a byte swap!
*/

void print_quad (unsigned int x)
{
    unsigned char b1, b2, b3, b4;

    b4 = (x & 0xFF000000) >> 24;
    b3 = (x & 0x00FF0000) >> 16;
    b2 = (x & 0x0000FF00) >> 8;
    b1 = (x & 0x000000FF);
    printf ("%02x %02x %02x %02x", b1, b2, b3, b4);
    printf ("   (%03d.%03d.%03d.%03d)", b1, b2, b3, b4);
    printf ("\n");
}
```

Chapter 22

Sockets - Ports and Protocols

22.1 Lab 1: Addresses, Services and Protocols

- Write a program to take three parameters:

  - An IP address in dot-quad notation or a host name
  - A service name or a port number
  - A protocol name (**tcp** or **udp**)

- From this information configure a `sockaddr_in` address structure. Test with parameters `localhost`, `www`, and `tcp`. You should get:

```
sin_family =            2
sin_addr   =   2130706433 (0x7F000001) (127.0.0.1)
sin_port   =           80 (0x00000050)
```

lab1_address.c

```c
#include <stdio.h>
#include <stdlib.h>
#include <errno.h>
#include <string.h>
#include <unistd.h>

#include <sys/types.h>
#include <sys/socket.h>
#include <netinet/in.h>
#include <netdb.h>
#include <arpa/inet.h>

#define DEFAULT_HOST        "localhost"
#define DEFAULT_SERVICE     "http"
#define DEFAULT_PROTOCOL    "tcp"

static int resolve (const char *host, const char *service, const char *proto,
                    struct sockaddr_in *addr);

int main (int argc, char *argv[])
{
    char *host = DEFAULT_HOST;
    char *service = DEFAULT_SERVICE;
    char *protocol = DEFAULT_PROTOCOL;
    struct sockaddr_in addr;
    unsigned short port;
    unsigned long address;
    int err;

    if (argc > 1)
        host = argv[1];

    if (argc > 2)
        service = argv[2];

    if (argc > 3)
        protocol = argv[3];

    err = resolve (host, service, protocol, &addr);

    if (!err) {
        port = ntohs (addr.sin_port);
        address = ntohl (addr.sin_addr.s_addr);
        printf ("sin_family = %12d\n", addr.sin_family);
        printf ("sin_addr   = %12lu (0x%08lX) (%s)\n", address, address,
                inet_ntoa (addr.sin_addr));
        printf ("sin_port   = %12hu (0x%08hX)\n", port, port);
    }
    return err;
}

static int
resolve (const char *host, const char *service, const char *proto,
         struct sockaddr_in *addr)
{
```

```
    unsigned short port;
    struct hostent *hostentry = NULL;
    struct servent *serventry = NULL;
    extern int h_errno;

    addr->sin_family = AF_INET;

    if (!(hostentry = gethostbyname (host))) {
        herror (host);
        return h_errno;
    }
    memcpy (&addr->sin_addr, hostentry->h_addr, hostentry->h_length);

    /* assume service was specified by port number */
    port = (unsigned short)atoi (service);

    if (port > 0) {
        /* success: service port specified by number */
        addr->sin_port = htons (port);
    } else {
        /* failed: service was probably specified by name, look it up */
        serventry = getservbyname (service, proto);

        if (serventry == NULL) {
            fprintf (stderr, "Failed to get service port: %s\n", service);
            return 1;
        }
        addr->sin_port = serventry->s_port;
    }

    return 0;
}

/* end of main */
```

22.2 Lab 2: Getting Services

- Write a program that takes as arguments a **service** and a **port number**; e.g., you can test your program with something like:

  ```
  lab finger 80
  ```

  (Note: The service and port number need not agree.)

- Use getservbyname() to find out what port number is bound to the service. Do this for both **TCP** and **UDP**.

- Use getservbyport() to find out what service is bound to the port number. Do this for both **TCP** and **UDP**.

- In both cases, print out any aliases for the service name.

lab2_serv_port.c

```c
/* Copyright 2009, J Cooperstein coop@coopj.com (GPLv2) */

#include <stdio.h>
#include <stdlib.h>
#include <string.h>
#include <errno.h>
#include <sys/socket.h>
#include <netinet/in.h>
#include <arpa/inet.h>
#include <netdb.h>

#define DEATH(mess) { perror(mess); exit(errno); }

void printit (struct servent *s);

int main (int argc, char *argv[])
{
    struct servent *result;
    char proto[4];
    short inport;
    int k;

    if (argc < 3) {
        printf ("\nUSAGE: %s Service PortNumber\n", argv[0]);
        exit (EXIT_FAILURE);
    }

    inport = (short)atoi (argv[2]);

    printf ("\nChecking things out for service = %s, port = %d\n\n",
            argv[1], inport);

    strcpy (proto, "tcp");

    for (k = 0; k < 2; k++) {
        if (k > 0)
            strcpy (proto, "udp");

        printf ("\n    Doing getservbyname for proto = %s\n\n", proto);
        if (!(result = getservbyname (argv[1], proto)))
            DEATH ("getservbyname");

        printit (result);

        printf ("\n    Doing getservbyport for proto = %s\n\n", proto);

        if (!(result = getservbyport (htons (inport), proto)))
            DEATH ("getservbyport");

        printit (result);
    }
    exit (EXIT_SUCCESS);
}

void printit (struct servent *s)
```

```
{
    int j;
    char **tmp;
    printf ("name = %15s,    port = %5d,    proto = %4s\n",
            s->s_name, ntohs (s->s_port), s->s_proto);

    if (*s->s_aliases) {
        for (j = 0, tmp = s->s_aliases; *tmp != NULL; j++, tmp++)
            printf ("  aliases[%d] = %s ", j, *tmp);
        printf ("\n");
    }
}
```

22.3   Lab 3: Getting All Services

- Write a program that lists all services, together with their port numbers, possible protocols,
  and aliases, on your local machine.

lab3_services.c

```
/* Copyright 2009, J Cooperstein coop@coopj.com (GPLv2) */

#include <stdio.h>
#include <stdlib.h>
#include <netdb.h>

void printit (struct servent *s);

int main (int argc, char *argv[])
{
    struct servent *result;

    setservent (0);

    while ((result = getservent ()))
        printit (result);

    endservent ();

    exit (EXIT_SUCCESS);
}

void printit (struct servent *s)
{
    int j;
    char **tmp;
    printf ("name = %15s,    port = %5d,    proto = %4s\n",
            s->s_name, ntohs (s->s_port), s->s_proto);

    if (*s->s_aliases) {
        for (j = 0, tmp = s->s_aliases; *tmp != NULL; j++, tmp++)
            printf ("  aliases[%d] = %s ", j, *tmp);
```

```
        printf ("\n");
    }
}
```

Chapter 23

Sockets - Clients

23.1 Lab 1: Simple Internet echo Client

- Take the sample Internet **echo** client program, and make it more robust, checking for errors at each stage, such as creating the socket, connecting to it, and reading and writing from it.

- Try it first on your local machine. (Make sure the **echo** server is on with `chkconfig --list | grep echo`)

  To work with other machines you may also have to open up your firewall to the echo port.

- Once it is turned it on you should be able to run it with:

  `lab1_echo_client localhost`

- Try running it on any other Internet address you think the **echo** server might be running on. What happens if it is not?

lab1_echo_client.c

```c
#include <stdio.h>
#include <stdlib.h>
#include <errno.h>
#include <unistd.h>
#include <string.h>
#include <sys/types.h>
#include <sys/socket.h>
#include <netinet/in.h>
#include <netdb.h>

#define MSG_LEN 1024
#define PORT_NUMBER 7
#define DEATH(mess) { perror(mess); exit(errno); }

int main (int argc, char **argv)
{
    int sd, msg_len;
    char message[MSG_LEN];
    struct sockaddr_in addr;
    struct hostent *hostent;

    if (argc < 2) {
        printf ("USAGE: %s host\n", argv[0]);
        exit (EXIT_FAILURE);
    }

    if ((sd = socket (PF_INET, SOCK_STREAM, 0)) < 0)
        DEATH (" Can't open a socket");

    printf ("Opened the socket just fine\n");

    if (!(hostent = gethostbyname (argv[1])))
        DEATH ("Can't get host");

    printf ("Got the host just fine\n");

    addr.sin_family = AF_INET;
    addr.sin_port = htons (PORT_NUMBER);
    memcpy (&addr.sin_addr, hostent->h_addr, hostent->h_length);

    if (connect (sd, (struct sockaddr *)&addr, sizeof (addr)))
        DEATH ("Can't connect to host");

    printf ("Connected to the host just fine\n");

    printf ("\nType in a message to send to %s\n\n", argv[1]);

    msg_len = strlen (fgets (message, MSG_LEN, stdin));
    if (write (sd, message, msg_len) < 0)
        DEATH ("Failed writing to the socket");

    memset (message, 0, MSG_LEN);
    printf
        ("\nCleared the message, am going to read it back from the socket\n\n");
    msg_len = read (sd, message, MSG_LEN);
```

```
    if (msg_len < 0)
        DEATH ("Failed reading from the socket");

    write (STDOUT_FILENO, message, msg_len);

    close (sd);
    exit (0);
}
```

23.2   Lab 2: Simple Internet finger Client

- Write a client that connects to the **finger** socket on some host, asks it for information and displays what it returns.

- You can look in /etc/services to find out the **finger** socket's port.

- You might get information on all users or only selected users.

- A naked carriage return sent to the **finger** server will return information on all logged in users (if the host will allow it). A user name followed by a carriage return will return information on that user.

- The sample solution is written to work with this usage:

  ```
  lab2_finger_client host user1 user2 ....
  ```

- Try it on the local host, and if you know any Internet sites where **finger** is still running, try there. If you want to be fancy you can get it to work with the standard **finger** syntax:

  ```
  finger user1@host1 user2@host2
  finger @host1 @host2
  ```

- **Note:** By default the **finger** server may not be installed, and if it is it may not be enabled. To take care of both steps, one could do (as root):

  ```
  yum install finger-server
  chkconfig finger on
  service xinetd restart
  ```

lab2_finger_client.c

```
/* Copyright 2009, J Cooperstein coop@coopj.com (GPLv2) */

#include <stdio.h>
#include <stdlib.h>
#include <errno.h>
#include <unistd.h>
#include <string.h>
#include <sys/types.h>
#include <sys/socket.h>
#include <netinet/in.h>
#include <netdb.h>
```

```
#define MSG_LEN 1024
#define PORT_NUMBER 79              /* finger port -- see /etc/services */

#define DEATH(mess) { perror(mess); exit(errno); }

int main (int argc, char **argv)
{
    int sd, msg_len;
    char message[MSG_LEN] = "";
    struct sockaddr_in addr;
    struct hostent *hostent;

    /* Parse the input arguments. */

    if (argc <= 1) {
        printf ("Usage: %s hostname <user1 user2 ...> \n", argv[0]);
        exit (0);
    }

    if (argc == 2) {
        strcpy (message, "\n");
    } else {
        int i;
        for (i = 2; i < argc; i++) {
            strcat (message, argv[i]);
            strcat (message, " ");
        }
        strcat (message, "\n");
    }

    if (!(hostent = gethostbyname (argv[1])))
        DEATH ("Can't get host");

    printf ("Got the host just fine\n");

    addr.sin_family = AF_INET;
    addr.sin_port = htons (PORT_NUMBER);
    memcpy (&addr.sin_addr, hostent->h_addr, hostent->h_length);

    /* open the socket and connect */

    if ((sd = socket (PF_INET, SOCK_STREAM, 0)) < 0)
        DEATH (" Can't open a socket");

    if (connect (sd, (struct sockaddr *)&addr, sizeof (addr)))
        DEATH ("Can't connect to host");

    printf ("Successfully Connected to: %s\n", argv[1]);

    /* send the command */

    if (write (sd, message, strlen (message)) < 0)
        DEATH ("Failed writing to the socket");
```

```
    /* clear the message and read back the response */

    memset (message, 0, MSG_LEN);
    msg_len = read (sd, message, MSG_LEN);

    if (msg_len < 0)
        DEATH ("Failed reading from the socket");

    write (STDOUT_FILENO, message, msg_len);

    close (sd);
    exit (EXIT_SUCCESS);
}
```

Chapter 24

Sockets - Servers

24.1   Lab 1: Unix Client/Server with UDP.

- Take the examples given for simple Unix domain socket **TCP** client and server programs (which can be found in the `SOLUTIONS/EXAMPLES` subdirectory tree) and convert them to work with **UDP**.

- Once the server is running, any line of input typed to the client is merely echoed back by the server, and then the client terminates.

- Test this by starting the server in one window, and then running the client in another. Try this first with the unaltered **TCP** programs, and then move on to your modified **UDP** ones.

- Now test by starting two instances of the client, and then sending output first from the second one started, and then from the first one. In what order does the server get the input?

- Do the same test with the **TCP** server examples. Are the results the same, or is the order inverted? Explain.

`lab1_unix_udp_client.c`

```
/* Copyright 2009, J Cooperstein coop@coopj.com (GPLv2) */

#include <stdlib.h>
#include <stdio.h>
#include <unistd.h>
#include <sys/socket.h>
#include <sys/un.h>

#define MSG_LEN 1024

int main (void)
{
    struct sockaddr_un uaddr;
    int msg_len, sd;
    char message[MSG_LEN];

    uaddr.sun_family = AF_UNIX;
    strcpy (uaddr.sun_path, "/tmp/mysock");

    sd = socket (PF_UNIX, SOCK_DGRAM, 0);
    connect (sd, (struct sockaddr *)&uaddr, sizeof (uaddr));

    msg_len = strlen (fgets (message, MSG_LEN, stdin));
    write (sd, message, msg_len);

    close (sd);
    exit (EXIT_SUCCESS);
}
```

lab1_unix_udp_server.c

```
/* Copyright 2009, J Cooperstein coop@coopj.com (GPLv2) */

#include <stdlib.h>
#include <stdio.h>
#include <unistd.h>
#include <sys/socket.h>
#include <sys/un.h>

#define MSG_LEN 1024

int main (void)
{
    struct sockaddr_un uaddr;
    int rc, sd;
    char message[MSG_LEN];

    uaddr.sun_family = AF_UNIX;
    strcpy (uaddr.sun_path, "/tmp/mysock");

    sd = socket (PF_UNIX, SOCK_DGRAM, 0);
    unlink ("/tmp/mysock");
    bind (sd, (struct sockaddr *)&uaddr, sizeof (uaddr));

    for (;;) {
```

```
        rc = read (sd, message, sizeof (message));
        write (STDOUT_FILENO, message, rc);
    }

    close (sd);
    exit (EXIT_SUCCESS);
}
```

24.2   Lab 2: Internet Client/Server with UDP.

- Now the take the example Internet client and server programs and convert them from **TCP** to **UDP**. Test in the same way you did for the Unix domain socket programs.

- Can your client program read back from the socket what it wrote to it? Try tracing your client with

  `strace client localhost`

  and try to see in detail what is happening.

lab2_inet_udp_client.c

```
/* Copyright 2009, J Cooperstein coop@coopj.com (GPLv2) */

#include <stdio.h>
#include <stdlib.h>
#include <errno.h>
#include <unistd.h>
#include <string.h>
#include <sys/types.h>
#include <sys/socket.h>
#include <netinet/in.h>
#include <netdb.h>
#define MSG_LEN 1024
#define PORT_NUMBER 7177

int main (int argc, char **argv)
{
    int sd, msg_len;
    char message[MSG_LEN];
    struct sockaddr_in addr;
    struct hostent *hostent;

    sd = socket (PF_INET, SOCK_DGRAM, 0);

    hostent = gethostbyname (argv[1]);
    addr.sin_family = AF_INET;
    addr.sin_port = htons (PORT_NUMBER);
    memcpy (&addr.sin_addr, hostent->h_addr, hostent->h_length);

    connect (sd, (struct sockaddr *)&addr, sizeof (addr));

    msg_len = strlen (fgets (message, MSG_LEN, stdin));
```

```
    write (sd, message, msg_len);

    memset (message, 0, MSG_LEN);
    msg_len = read (sd, message, MSG_LEN);
    write (STDOUT_FILENO, message, msg_len);

    close (sd);
    exit (0);
}
```

lab2_inet_udp_server.c

```
/* Copyright 2009, J Cooperstein coop@coopj.com (GPLv2) */

#include <stdlib.h>
#include <stdio.h>
#include <unistd.h>
#include <string.h>
#include <sys/socket.h>
#include <netinet/in.h>
#include <netdb.h>
#include <arpa/inet.h>

#define MSG_LEN 1024
#define PORT_NUMBER 7177

int main (void)
{
    struct sockaddr_in addr;
    int rc, sd, yes = 1;
    char message[MSG_LEN];

    addr.sin_family = AF_INET;
    addr.sin_addr.s_addr = htonl (INADDR_ANY);
    addr.sin_port = htons (PORT_NUMBER);

    sd = socket (PF_INET, SOCK_DGRAM, 0);

    setsockopt (sd, SOL_SOCKET, SO_REUSEADDR, &yes, sizeof (yes));
    bind (sd, (struct sockaddr *)&addr, sizeof (addr));

    for (;;) {

        rc = read (sd, message, sizeof (message));
        write (STDOUT_FILENO, message, rc);
        write (sd, message, rc);

        printf ("Received the end of input\n\n");
    }

    close (sd);
    exit (EXIT_SUCCESS);
}
```

Chapter 25

Sockets - Input/Output Operations

25.1   Lab 1: Using send() and recv()

- Take the examples given for simple Unix domain socket stream client and server programs and convert them to work with send() and recv().

- Test them as usual.

- This may seem a little more than necessary but we are going to use the codes in the following labs.

`lab1_unix_stream_c.c`

```
/* Copyright 2009, J Cooperstein coop@coopj.com (GPLv2) */
#include <stdlib.h>
#include <stdio.h>
#include <unistd.h>
#include <sys/socket.h>
#include <sys/un.h>
```

```
#define MSG_LEN 1024

int main (void)
{
    struct sockaddr_un uaddr;
    int msg_len, sd;
    char message[MSG_LEN];

    uaddr.sun_family = AF_UNIX;
    strcpy (uaddr.sun_path, "/tmp/mysock");

    sd = socket (PF_UNIX, SOCK_STREAM, 0);
    connect (sd, (struct sockaddr *)&uaddr, sizeof (uaddr));

    msg_len = strlen (fgets (message, MSG_LEN, stdin));
    send (sd, message, msg_len, 0);

    close (sd);
    exit (EXIT_SUCCESS);
}
```

lab1_unix_stream_s.c

```
 /* Copyright 2009, J Cooperstein coop@coopj.com (GPLv2) */
#include <stdlib.h>
#include <stdio.h>
#include <unistd.h>
#include <sys/socket.h>
#include <sys/un.h>

#define MSG_LEN 1024

int main (void)
{
    struct sockaddr_un uaddr;
    int rc, sd, cd;
    socklen_t alen = sizeof (struct sockaddr_un);
    char message[MSG_LEN];

    uaddr.sun_family = AF_UNIX;
    strcpy (uaddr.sun_path, "/tmp/mysock");

    sd = socket (PF_UNIX, SOCK_STREAM, 0);
    unlink ("/tmp/mysock");
    bind (sd, (struct sockaddr *)&uaddr, sizeof (uaddr));
    listen (sd, 5);

    for (;;) {

        cd = accept (sd, NULL, &alen);

        rc = recv (cd, message, sizeof (message), 0);
        write (STDOUT_FILENO, message, rc);

        close (cd);
```

```
    }

    close (sd);
    exit (EXIT_SUCCESS);
}
```

lab1_inet_stream_c.c

```
/* Copyright 2009, J Cooperstein coop@coopj.com (GPLv2) */

#include <stdio.h>
#include <stdlib.h>
#include <errno.h>
#include <unistd.h>
#include <string.h>
#include <sys/types.h>
#include <sys/socket.h>
#include <netinet/in.h>
#include <netdb.h>
#define MSG_LEN 1024
#define PORT_NUMBER 7177

int main (int argc, char **argv)
{
    int sd, msg_len;
    char message[MSG_LEN];
    struct sockaddr_in addr;
    struct hostent *hostent;

    sd = socket (PF_INET, SOCK_STREAM, 0);

    hostent = gethostbyname (argv[1]);
    addr.sin_family = AF_INET;
    addr.sin_port = htons (PORT_NUMBER);
    memcpy (&addr.sin_addr, hostent->h_addr, hostent->h_length);

    connect (sd, (struct sockaddr *)&addr, sizeof (addr));

    msg_len = strlen (fgets (message, MSG_LEN, stdin));
    send (sd, message, msg_len, 0);

    memset (message, 0, MSG_LEN);
    msg_len = recv (sd, message, MSG_LEN, 0);
    write (STDOUT_FILENO, message, msg_len);

    close (sd);
    exit (EXIT_SUCCESS);
}
```

lab1_inet_stream_s.c

```
/* Copyright 2009, J Cooperstein coop@coopj.com (GPLv2) */

#include <stdlib.h>
```

```c
#include <stdio.h>
#include <unistd.h>
#include <string.h>
#include <sys/socket.h>
#include <netinet/in.h>
#include <netdb.h>
#include <arpa/inet.h>

#define MSG_LEN 1024
#define PORT_NUMBER 7177

int main (void)
{
    struct sockaddr_in addr, con_addr;
    int rc, sd, cd, yes = 1;
    socklen_t alen = sizeof (struct sockaddr_in);
    char message[MSG_LEN];

    addr.sin_family = AF_INET;
    addr.sin_addr.s_addr = htonl (INADDR_ANY);
    addr.sin_port = htons (PORT_NUMBER);

    sd = socket (PF_INET, SOCK_STREAM, 0);

    setsockopt (sd, SOL_SOCKET, SO_REUSEADDR, &yes, sizeof (yes));
    bind (sd, (struct sockaddr *)&addr, sizeof (addr));
    listen (sd, 5);

    for (;;) {

        printf ("\nAccepting input on port %d\n", PORT_NUMBER);
        cd = accept (sd, (struct sockaddr *)&con_addr, &alen);

        rc = recv (cd, message, sizeof (message), 0);
        write (STDOUT_FILENO, message, rc);
        rc = send (cd, message, rc, 0);

        printf ("Received the end of input\n\n");
        close (cd);
    }

    close (sd);
    exit (EXIT_SUCCESS);
}
```

25.2   Lab 2: Using sendto() and recvfrom() for TCP.

- Take your Internet solutions for the previous problem and convert them to work with sendto() and recvfrom(), and test them as usual.

- For extra work, do the same thing with the Unix domain sockets. Does this work?

`lab2_inet_stream_sr_c.c`

```
/* Copyright 2009, J Cooperstein coop@coopj.com (GPLv2) */
#include <stdio.h>
#include <stdlib.h>
#include <errno.h>
#include <unistd.h>
#include <string.h>
#include <sys/types.h>
#include <sys/socket.h>
#include <netinet/in.h>
#include <netdb.h>
#define MSG_LEN 1024
#define PORT_NUMBER 7177

int main (int argc, char **argv)
{
    int sd, msg_len, rc;
    char message[MSG_LEN];
    struct sockaddr_in addr;
    socklen_t alen = sizeof (struct sockaddr_in);
    struct hostent *hostent;

    sd = socket (PF_INET, SOCK_STREAM, 0);

    hostent = gethostbyname (argv[1]);
    addr.sin_family = AF_INET;
    addr.sin_port = htons (PORT_NUMBER);
    memcpy (&addr.sin_addr, hostent->h_addr, hostent->h_length);

    connect (sd, (struct sockaddr *)&addr, sizeof (addr));

    msg_len = strlen (fgets (message, MSG_LEN, stdin));
    sendto (sd, message, msg_len, 0, (struct sockaddr *)&addr, sizeof (addr));

    memset (message, 0, MSG_LEN);
    rc = recvfrom (sd, message, MSG_LEN, 0, (struct sockaddr *)&addr, &alen);

    write (STDOUT_FILENO, message, rc);

    close (sd);
    exit (EXIT_SUCCESS);
}
```

lab2_inet_stream_sr_s.c

```
/* Copyright 2009, J Cooperstein coop@coopj.com (GPLv2) */
#include <stdlib.h>
#include <stdio.h>
#include <unistd.h>
#include <string.h>
#include <sys/socket.h>
#include <netinet/in.h>
#include <netdb.h>
#include <arpa/inet.h>

#define MSG_LEN 1024
```

```
#define PORT_NUMBER 7177

int main (void)
{
    struct sockaddr_in addr, con_addr;
    int rc, sd, cd, yes = 1;
    socklen_t alen = sizeof (struct sockaddr_in);
    char message[MSG_LEN];

    addr.sin_family = AF_INET;
    addr.sin_addr.s_addr = htonl (INADDR_ANY);
    addr.sin_port = htons (PORT_NUMBER);

    sd = socket (PF_INET, SOCK_STREAM, 0);

    setsockopt (sd, SOL_SOCKET, SO_REUSEADDR, &yes, sizeof (yes));
    bind (sd, (struct sockaddr *)&addr, sizeof (addr));
    listen (sd, 5);

    for (;;) {

        printf ("\nAccepting input on port %d\n", PORT_NUMBER);
        cd = accept (sd, (struct sockaddr *)&con_addr, &alen);

        rc = recvfrom (cd, message, sizeof (message), 0,
                        (struct sockaddr *)&con_addr, &alen);
        write (STDOUT_FILENO, message, rc);
        sendto (cd, message, rc, 0, (struct sockaddr *)&con_addr, alen);

        printf ("Received the end of input\n\n");
        close (cd);
    }

    close (sd);
    exit (EXIT_SUCCESS);
}
```

25.3   Lab 3: Using sendto() and recvfrom() for datagrams.

- Now provide solutions for both Unix domain and Internet sockets that work with sendto() and recvfrom(), and test them as usual.

lab3_unix_dgram_c.c

```
 /* Copyright 2009, J Cooperstein coop@coopj.com (GPLv2) */
#include <stdlib.h>
#include <stdio.h>
#include <unistd.h>
#include <sys/socket.h>
#include <sys/un.h>

#define MSG_LEN 1024
```

```
int main (void)
{
    struct sockaddr_un uaddr;
    int msg_len, sd;
    char message[MSG_LEN];

    uaddr.sun_family = AF_UNIX;
    strcpy (uaddr.sun_path, "/tmp/mysock");

    sd = socket (PF_UNIX, SOCK_DGRAM, 0);

    msg_len = strlen (fgets (message, MSG_LEN, stdin));
    sendto (sd, message, msg_len, 0, (struct sockaddr *)&uaddr, sizeof (uaddr));

    close (sd);
    exit (EXIT_SUCCESS);
}
```

lab3_unix_dgram_s.c

```
 /* Copyright 2009, J Cooperstein coop@coopj.com (GPLv2) */
#include <stdlib.h>
#include <stdio.h>
#include <unistd.h>
#include <sys/socket.h>
#include <sys/un.h>

#define MSG_LEN 1024

int main (void)
{
    struct sockaddr_un addr;
    int rc, sd;
    socklen_t alen = sizeof (struct sockaddr_un);
    char message[MSG_LEN];

    addr.sun_family = AF_UNIX;
    strcpy (addr.sun_path, "/tmp/mysock");

    sd = socket (PF_UNIX, SOCK_DGRAM, 0);
    unlink ("/tmp/mysock");
    bind (sd, (struct sockaddr *)&addr, sizeof (addr));

    for (;;) {
        rc = recvfrom (sd, message, sizeof (message), 0,
                        (struct sockaddr *)&addr, &alen);
        write (STDOUT_FILENO, message, rc);
    }

    close (sd);
    exit (EXIT_SUCCESS);
}
```

lab3_inet_dgram_c.c

```c
/* Copyright 2009, J Cooperstein coop@coopj.com (GPLv2) */
#include <stdio.h>
#include <stdlib.h>
#include <errno.h>
#include <unistd.h>
#include <string.h>
#include <sys/types.h>
#include <sys/socket.h>
#include <netinet/in.h>
#include <netdb.h>
#define MSG_LEN 1024
#define PORT_NUMBER 7177

int main (int argc, char **argv)
{
    int sd, msg_len, rc;
    char message[MSG_LEN];
    struct sockaddr_in addr, from_addr;
    struct hostent *hostent;
    socklen_t alen = sizeof (struct sockaddr_in);

    sd = socket (PF_INET, SOCK_DGRAM, 0);

    hostent = gethostbyname (argv[1]);
    addr.sin_family = AF_INET;
    addr.sin_port = htons (PORT_NUMBER);
    memcpy (&addr.sin_addr, hostent->h_addr, hostent->h_length);

    msg_len = strlen (fgets (message, MSG_LEN, stdin));
    sendto (sd, message, msg_len, 0, (struct sockaddr *)&addr, sizeof (addr));

    memset (message, 0, MSG_LEN);

    rc = recvfrom (sd, message, MSG_LEN, 0, (struct sockaddr *)&from_addr,
                   &alen);
    write (STDOUT_FILENO, message, rc);

    close (sd);
    exit (EXIT_SUCCESS);
}
```

lab3_inet_dgram_s.c

```c
/* Copyright 2009, J Cooperstein coop@coopj.com (GPLv2) */
#include <stdlib.h>
#include <stdio.h>
#include <unistd.h>
#include <string.h>
#include <sys/socket.h>
#include <netinet/in.h>
#include <netdb.h>
#include <arpa/inet.h>

#define MSG_LEN 1024
#define PORT_NUMBER 7177
```

```
int main (void)
{
    struct sockaddr_in addr;
    int rc, sd, yes = 1;
    socklen_t addr_len = sizeof (struct sockaddr_in);
    char message[MSG_LEN];

    addr_len = sizeof (addr);

    addr.sin_family = AF_INET;
    addr.sin_addr.s_addr = htonl (INADDR_ANY);
    addr.sin_port = htons (PORT_NUMBER);

    sd = socket (PF_INET, SOCK_DGRAM, 0);

    setsockopt (sd, SOL_SOCKET, SO_REUSEADDR, &yes, sizeof (yes));
    bind (sd, (struct sockaddr *)&addr, sizeof (addr));

    for (;;) {

        printf ("\nAccepting input on port %d\n", PORT_NUMBER);

        rc = recvfrom (sd, message, sizeof (message), 0,
                       (struct sockaddr *)&addr, &addr_len);
        write (STDOUT_FILENO, message, rc);
        sendto (sd, message, rc, 0, (struct sockaddr *)&addr, sizeof (addr));

        printf ("Received the end of input\n\n");
    }

    close (sd);
    exit (EXIT_SUCCESS);
}
```

25.4   Lab 4: Using sendfile().

- Write a program that opens a file and copies it to a socket, using **TCP** over the Internet. Use port 7177 as before, and by default you can connect to the localhost.

- In order to do this you'll also need a server program to receive the data. You can adopt the previous Internet **TCP** server to do this. You just need to make the modifications that the data read go to an output file, and that it not write back to the client.

- The input file (called `infile` by default) can be first filled with zeros, with a command like:

  ```
  dd if=/dev/zero of=infile bs=1024 count=8192
  ```

  which would create an 8 MB file.

- You may do the I/O in a number of chunks (given by the third argument, which can be 1 by default), and repeat the whole operation a number of times given by the fourth argument (perhaps 10 by default) in order to produce better averaged timing information.

- Now make small adaptations to the program to have it use **sendfile()** instead of the **read()** / **write()** combination in the first program.

- In our sample solution, we have combined this into one program which takes as its first argument either **on** or **off**. You can compare the performance of the two methods by starting the server program and then doing:

```
time lab4_sendfile_client off [infile] [hostname] [nchunks] [nreps]
time lab4_sendfile client on  [infile] [hostname] [nchunks] [nreps]
```

  and comparing the results.

- You'll probably want to do this several times, making sure your system is lightly loaded. The **time** command will report on real (or wall clock), user, and system time. The system time may not be reliable, so to be rough, just concentrate on the wall clock.

- If you want to get fancier you can put timing instrumentation in your code using **gettimeofday()** or a similar function.

- **Note:** It is quite possible your timings will be limited by disk I/O and not the network transmission. In order to make sure this is not the case, work with a **ram disk**. You can do this by:

```
mkdir ramdisk
mount -t tmpfs none ./ramdisk
```

  and then make sure your data file is on the ramdisk.

lab4_sendfile_client.c

```c
/* Copyright 2009, J Cooperstein coop@coopj.com (GPLv2) */

#include <stdio.h>
#include <stdlib.h>
#include <unistd.h>
#include <string.h>
#include <fcntl.h>

#include <sys/sendfile.h>

#include <sys/types.h>
#include <sys/socket.h>
#include <netinet/in.h>
#include <netdb.h>

#include <sys/time.h>

#define PORT_NUMBER 7177

#define GET_ELAPSED_TIME(tv1,tv2) ( \
  (double)( (tv2.tv_sec - tv1.tv_sec) \
          + .000001 * (tv2.tv_usec - tv1.tv_usec)))

int main (int argc, char *argv[])
{
```

```
char *buffer;
char hname[128] = "localhost", infile[128] = "./infile";
int rc, fd1, sd, j, k, size, nbuf, nchunk = 1, nrep = 10, which = 0;
struct sockaddr_in addr;
struct hostent *hostent;
struct timeval tv1, tv2;
double io_time = 0;

/* 1st arg = on or off for sendfile or read/write
   2nd arg = filename (./infile by default)
   3rd arg = hostname ("localhost" by default)
   4th arg = number of chunks (1 by default)
   5th arg = number of reps (10 by default) */

if (argc < 2) {
    fprintf (stderr, "USAGE: %s on | off "
            "[infile] [hostname] [nchunks] [nreps]", argv[0]);
    exit (-1);
}
if (!strncmp (argv[1], "on", 2))
    which = 1;

if (argc > 2)
    strcpy (infile, argv[2]);
if (argc > 3)
    strcpy (hname, argv[3]);
if (argc > 4)
    nchunk = atoi (argv[4]);
if (argc > 5)
    nrep = atoi (argv[5]);

/* get the file size and then determine the size of the buffers, chunks */

fd1 = open (infile, O_RDONLY);
size = (int)lseek (fd1, 0, SEEK_END);
close (fd1);
nbuf = (size - 1) / nchunk + 1;

/* malloc the input buffer */
buffer = malloc (nbuf);

printf ("Input file: %s,  Size: %d, Chunks: %d, Bytes: %d \n", infile,
        size, nchunk, nbuf);

hostent = gethostbyname (hname);
addr.sin_family = AF_INET;
addr.sin_port = htons (PORT_NUMBER);
memcpy (&addr.sin_addr, hostent->h_addr, hostent->h_length);

printf ("Doing iteration:");
for (k = 0; k < nrep; k++) {
    printf ("%4d", k + 1);
    fflush (stdout);
    fd1 = open (infile, O_RDONLY);
```

```
        sd = socket (PF_INET, SOCK_STREAM, 0);

        connect (sd, (struct sockaddr *)&addr, sizeof (addr));

        gettimeofday (&tv1, NULL);
        for (j = 0; j < nchunk; j++) {
            if (which == 0) {
                rc = read (fd1, buffer, nbuf);
                write (sd, buffer, rc);
            } else {
                off_t offset = j * nbuf;
                rc = sendfile (sd, fd1, &offset, nbuf);
            }
        }
        gettimeofday (&tv2, NULL);
        io_time += GET_ELAPSED_TIME (tv1, tv2);
        close (fd1);
        close (sd);
    }
    if (which == 0)
        fprintf (stderr, "\nDONE, Did Not Use sendfile()");
    else
        fprintf (stderr, "\nDONE, Did    Use sendfile()");
    printf ("\n Total time spent in I/O = %f seconds\n", io_time);
    exit (EXIT_SUCCESS);
}
```

lab4_sendfile_server.c

```
 /* Copyright 2009, J Cooperstein coop@coopj.com (GPLv2) */

#include <stdlib.h>
#include <stdio.h>
#include <unistd.h>
#include <string.h>
#include <fcntl.h>
#include <sys/socket.h>
#include <netinet/in.h>
#include <netdb.h>
#include <arpa/inet.h>

#define MSG_LEN 64*1024          /* limited by socket buffer size anyway */
#define PORT_NUMBER 7177

int main (void)
{
    struct sockaddr_in addr, con_addr;
    int rc, sd, cd, yes = 1, fd2, bytes_received;
    socklen_t alen = sizeof (struct sockaddr_in);
    char message[MSG_LEN];

    addr.sin_family = AF_INET;
    addr.sin_addr.s_addr = htonl (INADDR_ANY);
    addr.sin_port = htons (PORT_NUMBER);
```

```
        sd = socket (PF_INET, SOCK_STREAM, 0);

        setsockopt (sd, SOL_SOCKET, SO_REUSEADDR, &yes, sizeof (yes));
        bind (sd, (struct sockaddr *)&addr, sizeof (addr));
        listen (sd, 5);

        for (;;) {

            /* reopen the outfile each time so it doesn't grow large */

            cd = accept (sd, (struct sockaddr *)&con_addr, &alen);
            bytes_received = 0;

            /* reopen the outfile each time so it doesn't grow large */
            fd2 = open ("outfile", O_RDWR | O_CREAT | O_TRUNC, 0666);
            printf ("\nAccepting input on port %d\n", PORT_NUMBER);

            do {
                rc = recv (cd, message, sizeof (message), 0);
                bytes_received += rc;
                write (fd2, message, rc);
            } while (rc > 0);

            printf ("Received:  %d bytes\n", bytes_received);
            printf ("Received the end of input\n\n");
            close (cd);
            close (fd2);
        }

        close (sd);

        exit (EXIT_SUCCESS);
}
```

25.5   Lab 5: Using socketpair() on a socket

- Using socketpair() write a simple program that creates a pair of connected sockets.

- Write an identifying message into each socket, clear it, and then read from the socket.

- Print out what is sent to and read from the sockets. Are you getting full duplex operation?

lab5_socketpair.c

```
/* Copyright 2009, J Cooperstein coop@coopj.com (GPLv2) */

#include <stdio.h>
#include <stdlib.h>
#include <unistd.h>
#include <sys/types.h>
#include <sys/socket.h>
#include <string.h>
#include <errno.h>
```

```
#define STR_LEN 128

#define DEATH(mess) { perror(mess); exit(errno); }

int main (int argc, char *argv[])
{
    int j, rc, sv[2];
    char string[2][STR_LEN];

    if (socketpair (PF_LOCAL, SOCK_STREAM, 0, sv))
        DEATH ("Failed to make a socket pair");

    printf ("\n");
    for (j = 0; j < 2; j++) {
        sprintf (string[j], "This is the message going out on sv[%d]", j);
        printf ("Initial string %d is:          %s\n", j, string[j]);
        rc = write (sv[j], string[j], strlen (string[j]));
        printf ("     rc from write on %d is %d\n", j, rc);
        memset (&string[j], 0, STR_LEN);
    }

    printf ("\n");
    for (j = 0; j < 2; j++)
        printf ("After clear, string %d is:      %s\n", j, string[j]);

    printf ("\n");
    for (j = 0; j < 2; j++) {
        rc = read (sv[j], string[j], STR_LEN);
        printf ("     rc from read  on %d is %d\n", j, rc);
        printf ("After read back, string %d is: %s\n", j, string[j]);
        close (sv[j]);
    }
    printf ("\n");

    exit (EXIT_SUCCESS);
}
```

Chapter 26

Sockets - Options

26.1   Lab 1: Examining socket options

- Write a program that uses getsockopt() to examine the default options for a **TCP/IP** socket.

- Just open a socket (you don't have to do anything with it, like connecting), and then using the option names available in **/usr/src/linux/arch/x86/include/asm/socket.h**, obtain their values.

- Note that most of the options have an integer value, but some are not, such as those which are given in a timeval data structure.

- Print out the symbolic name along with the integer option number.

- For the above you'll use SOL_SOCKET for the level parameter. You can also try other values such as SOL_IP. Look at the **man** pages for **socket(7), tcp(7), ip(7), unix(7)**, etc. to get some ideas.

lab1_options.c

```c
/* Copyright 2009, J Cooperstein coop@coopj.com (GPLv2) */

#include <stdio.h>
#include <stdlib.h>
#include <errno.h>
#include <unistd.h>
#include <string.h>
#include <sys/types.h>
#include <sys/socket.h>

#define DEATH(mess) { perror(mess); exit(errno); }

void doit_int (int sd, int optname, char *name)
{
    socklen_t optlen = sizeof (int);
    int val;
    if (getsockopt (sd, SOL_SOCKET, optname, &val, &optlen))
        fprintf (stderr, "getsockopt failed for: %32s (%2d)", name, optname);
    else
        printf ("%15s (%2d)  optlen=%d  value:%6d\n", name, optname,
                optlen, val);
}

void doit_timeval (int sd, int optname, char *name)
{
    socklen_t optlen = sizeof (struct timeval);
    struct timeval val;
    if (getsockopt (sd, SOL_SOCKET, optname, &val, &optlen))
        fprintf (stderr, "getsockopt failed for: %32s", name);
    else
        printf ("%15s (%2d)  optlen=%d  value: %d secs %d usecs\n", name,
                optname, optlen, (int)val.tv_sec, (int)val.tv_usec);
}

int main (int argc, char **argv)
{
    int sd;

    if ((sd = socket (PF_INET, SOCK_STREAM, 0)) < 0)
        DEATH ("Couldn't open socket");

    doit_int (sd, SO_DEBUG, "SO_DEBUG");
    doit_int (sd, SO_REUSEADDR, "SO_REUSEADDR");
    doit_int (sd, SO_TYPE, "SO_TYPE");
    doit_int (sd, SO_ERROR, "SO_ERROR");
    doit_int (sd, SO_DONTROUTE, "SO_DONTROUTE");
    doit_int (sd, SO_BROADCAST, "SO_BROADCAST");
    doit_int (sd, SO_SNDBUF, "SO_SNDBUF");
    doit_int (sd, SO_RCVBUF, "SO_RCVBUF");
    doit_int (sd, SO_KEEPALIVE, "SO_KEEPALIVE");
    doit_int (sd, SO_OOBINLINE, "SO_OOBINLINE");
    doit_int (sd, SO_NO_CHECK, "SO_NO_CHECK");
    doit_int (sd, SO_PRIORITY, "SO_PRIORITY");
    doit_int (sd, SO_LINGER, "SO_LINGER");
    doit_int (sd, SO_BSDCOMPAT, "SO_BSDCOMPAT");
```

```
/* doit_int(sd, SO_REUSEPORT,"SO_REUSEPORT"); */
    doit_int (sd, SO_PASSCRED, "SO_PASSCRED");
    doit_int (sd, SO_PEERCRED, "SO_PEERCRED");
    doit_int (sd, SO_RCVLOWAT, "SO_RCVLOWAT");
    doit_int (sd, SO_SNDLOWAT, "SO_SNDLOWAT");
    doit_timeval (sd, SO_RCVTIMEO, "SO_RCVTIMEO");
    doit_timeval (sd, SO_SNDTIMEO, "SO_SNDTIMEO");
    doit_int (sd, SO_SECURITY_AUTHENTICATION, "SO_SECURITY_AUTHENTICATION");
    doit_int (sd, SO_SECURITY_ENCRYPTION_TRANSPORT,
             "SO_SECURITY_ENCRYPTION_TRANSPORT");
    doit_int (sd, SO_SECURITY_ENCRYPTION_NETWORK,
             "SO_SECURITY_ENCRYPTION_NETWORK");
    doit_int (sd, SO_BINDTODEVICE, "SO_BINDTODEVICE");
    doit_int (sd, SO_ATTACH_FILTER, "SO_ATTACH_FILTER");
    doit_int (sd, SO_DETACH_FILTER, "SO_DETACH_FILTER");
    doit_int (sd, SO_PEERNAME, "SO_PEERNAME");
    doit_int (sd, SO_TIMESTAMP, "SO_TIMESTAMP");
    doit_int (sd, SO_ACCEPTCONN, "SO_ACCEPTCONN");

    close (sd);
    exit (0);
}
```

Chapter 27

Netlink Sockets

27.1 Lab 1: Using Netlink to monitor routing changes.

- We give you a program which is capable of monitoring (through **netlink**) routing table operations: **lab1_nl_routing.c**. Compile and execute.

- Add, delete, and modify routes on your system and see how the program responds. If you stop and restart your network (with `service network restart`) you should see some messages. Or you can try some commands such as

  ```
  route add -net 192.56.76.0 netmask 255.255.255.0 dev eth0
  route add -host 123.213.221.231 eth0
  route add -net 10.13.21.0 netmask 255.255.255.0 gw 192.168.1.254 eth0
  ```

- If you are ambitious, modify the code to obtain more information about the requests.

lab1_nl_routing.c

```
/* Copyright 2009, J Cooperstein coop@coopj.com (GPLv2) */

/*
```

Netlink example that uses routing table operations to get feedback
from the kernel. Error handling code was skipped in order to reduce
code length.

Copyright Dominic Duval <dduval@redhat.com> according to the terms
of the GNU Public License.

```c
*/
#include <unistd.h>
#include <stdio.h>
#include <stdlib.h>
#include <string.h>
#include <netinet/in.h>
#include <sys/socket.h>
#include <linux/types.h>
#include <linux/netlink.h>
#include <linux/rtnetlink.h>

#define MAX_PAYLOAD 1024

int read_event (int sock)
{
    int ret;
    struct nlmsghdr *nlh;

    nlh = malloc (NLMSG_SPACE (MAX_PAYLOAD));
    memset (nlh, 0, NLMSG_SPACE (MAX_PAYLOAD));
    ret = recv (sock, (void *)nlh, NLMSG_SPACE (MAX_PAYLOAD), 0);

    switch (nlh->nlmsg_type) {
    case RTM_NEWROUTE:
        printf ("NEWROUTE\n");
        break;
    case RTM_DELROUTE:
        printf ("DELROUTE\n");
        break;
    case RTM_GETROUTE:
        printf ("GETROUTE\n");
        break;
    default:
        printf ("Unknown type\n");
        break;
    }
    return 0;
}

int main (int argc, char *argv[])
{
    int nls = socket (PF_NETLINK, SOCK_RAW, NETLINK_ROUTE);
    struct sockaddr_nl addr;

    memset ((void *)&addr, 0, sizeof (addr));

    addr.nl_family = AF_NETLINK;
    addr.nl_pid = getpid ();
    addr.nl_groups = RTMGRP_IPV4_ROUTE;
```

```
        bind (nls, (struct sockaddr *)&addr, sizeof (addr));

        while (1)
            read_event (nls);
        return 0;
}
```

27.2 Lab 2: Using Netlink to send kernel messages to an application.

- We give you a kernel module (**lab2_nl_sender.c**) that sends messages to a netlink socket to be monitored by a user application (**lab2_nl_receive_test.c**).

- Compile and test the two programs. Try sending multiple messages through straightforward modifications.

lab2_nl_sender.c

```
/* Copyright 2009, J Cooperstein coop@coopj.com (GPLv2) */
/*
  Netlink demo that sends a message from kernel-space to user-space.

  Copyright Dominic Duval <dduval@redhat.com> according to the terms
  of the GNU Public License.

 (minor changes introduced by J. Cooperstein, coop@coopj.com
  to work with newer kernels.)

 (major changes introduced by Paul Drews, paul.drews@intel.com)

*/

#include <linux/module.h>
#include <net/sock.h>
#include <linux/netlink.h>
#include <linux/sched.h>
#include <linux/jiffies.h>
#include <linux/kthread.h>

#define MAX_PAYLOAD 1024
#define NETLINK_MESSAGE "This message originated from the kernel!"
#define NL_EXAMPLE 19           /* was 19 */
#define NL_GROUP 1              /* was 1 */

#define MSG_INTERVAL_SEC 5

#define seconds_to_jiffies(sec) (cputime_to_jiffies(secs_to_cputime(sec)))

static struct sock *nl_sk = NULL;
static struct task_struct *sender_thread = NULL;

static int my_sender_thread (void *data)
```

```
{
    struct sk_buff *skb = NULL;
    struct nlmsghdr *nlh;

    do {
        skb = alloc_skb (NLMSG_SPACE (MAX_PAYLOAD), GFP_KERNEL);
        nlh = (struct nlmsghdr *)skb_put (skb, NLMSG_SPACE (MAX_PAYLOAD));
        nlh->nlmsg_len = NLMSG_SPACE (MAX_PAYLOAD);
        nlh->nlmsg_pid = 0;
        nlh->nlmsg_flags = 0;
        strcpy (NLMSG_DATA (nlh), NETLINK_MESSAGE);
        NETLINK_CB (skb).pid = 0;
/*      NETLINK_CB (skb).dst_pid = 0;   removed in 2.6.20 */
        NETLINK_CB (skb).dst_group = NL_GROUP;
        netlink_broadcast (nl_sk, skb, 0, NL_GROUP, GFP_KERNEL);
        printk (KERN_INFO "my_sender_thread sent a message at jiffies=%ld\n",
                jiffies);
        set_current_state (TASK_INTERRUPTIBLE);
        schedule_timeout (seconds_to_jiffies (MSG_INTERVAL_SEC));
    } while (!kthread_should_stop ());

    return 0;

}                               /* my_sender_thread */

static int __init my_init (void)
{
    nl_sk = netlink_kernel_create (&init_net, NL_EXAMPLE, 0, NULL, NULL,
                                   THIS_MODULE);

    if (nl_sk == NULL)
        return -1;

    sender_thread = kthread_run (my_sender_thread,
                                 NULL, "lab2_nl_sender_thread");
    if (IS_ERR (sender_thread)) {
        printk (KERN_INFO "Error %ld createing thread\n",
                PTR_ERR (sender_thread));
        sock_release (nl_sk->sk_socket);
        return -1;
    }

    printk (KERN_INFO "Adding netlink testing module\n");

    return 0;
}

static void __exit my_exit (void)
{
    printk (KERN_INFO "Removing netlink testing module\n");
    kthread_stop (sender_thread);
    sock_release (nl_sk->sk_socket);
}


module_exit (my_exit);
```

```
module_init (my_init);

MODULE_AUTHOR ("Dominic Duval");
MODULE_AUTHOR ("Paul Drews");
MODULE_AUTHOR ("Jerry Cooperstein");
MODULE_DESCRIPTION ("CLDD 1.0: lab2_nl_sender.c");
MODULE_LICENSE ("GPL v2");
```

lab2_nl_receive_test.c

```
/* Copyright 2009, J Cooperstein coop@coopj.com (GPLv2) */
/*
Netlink example that receives feedback from the kernel.
Error handling was skipped in order to reduce code length.

Copyright Dominic Duval <dduval@redhat.com> according to the terms
of the GNU Public License.

(minor changes introduced by J. Cooperstein, coop@coopj.com
  to work with newer kernels.)

*/
#include <errno.h>
#include <unistd.h>
#include <stdlib.h>
#include <string.h>
#include <stdio.h>
#include <netinet/in.h>
#include <sys/socket.h>
#include <linux/types.h>
#include <linux/netlink.h>
#include <linux/rtnetlink.h>

#define MAX_PAYLOAD 1024
#define NL_EXAMPLE 19          /* was 19 */
#define NL_GROUP 1             /* was 1 */

int read_event (int sock)
{
    int ret;
    struct nlmsghdr *nlh;

    nlh = malloc (NLMSG_SPACE (MAX_PAYLOAD));
    memset (nlh, 0, NLMSG_SPACE (MAX_PAYLOAD));
    ret = recv (sock, (void *)nlh, NLMSG_SPACE (MAX_PAYLOAD), 0);

    printf ("Message size: %d , Message: %s\n", ret, (char *)NLMSG_DATA (nlh));

    return 0;
}

int main (int argc, char *argv[])
{
    struct sockaddr_nl addr;
    int nls;
```

```
        int rc;

        /* Set up the netlink socket */
        nls = socket (PF_NETLINK, SOCK_RAW, NL_EXAMPLE);
        printf ("nls=%d\n", nls);

        memset ((void *)&addr, 0, sizeof (addr));
        addr.nl_family = AF_NETLINK;
        addr.nl_pid = getpid ();
        addr.nl_groups = NL_GROUP;
        rc = bind (nls, (struct sockaddr *)&addr, sizeof (addr));
        printf ("errno=%d\n", errno);
        perror ("bind");
        printf ("rc from bind = %d\n", rc);

        while (1)
            read_event (nls);

        return 0;
}
```

Chapter 28

Sockets - Multiplexing and Concurrent Servers

28.1   Lab 1: I/O Multiplexing and select()

- Write a program that takes some files names as arguments. It should open each file, and then scan each one for incoming data.

- When any file has data ready to read it should print out the filename as well as the data. Loop indefinitely, printing the data from each file as it comes.

- Test the program by creating two named pipes with the `mkfifo` command:

```
mkfifo file1
mkfifo file2
```

(we'll discuss this when we discuss **pipes**) and opening up three shell windows (or using three virtual terminals if you don't have **X** running).

- In two windows, type `cat > file1` and `cat > file2`; in the third window, run your program. You should be able to type "Hello" in the first window, and see "file1 says: Hello" come from your test program, then type "Goodbye" in the second window and see "file2 says: Goodbye", etc.

- Some hints:

  - Print out the name of each file as you open it. Remember that if you try to open a **fifo** for reading, and nobody has it open for writing, you will stop dead right there! This is an easy mistake to make and printing each filename you open will make it obvious when this happens.

  - You don't have to worry about files being closed if you don't want to. For extra credit, have your program "forget" about closed files when you hear that they are closed, but this can be tricky so don't worry about it if you don't want to.

  - Don't forget that the first argument to **select()** should be the highest file descriptor that is set in your file descriptor set **plus one**, not the number of files set! This is very important!

- Implement the program using **select()**.

- Implement the program using **epoll**.

lab1_select.c

```
/* Copyright 2009, J Cooperstein coop@coopj.com (GPLv2) */

#include <stdio.h>
#include <assert.h>
#include <unistd.h>
#include <fcntl.h>
#include <string.h>
#include <errno.h>
#include <stdlib.h>

#define MAX_CONNS 100
#define READ_AMT (4 * 1024)

/*
 * Read from several files at once.
 */
int main (int argc, char *argv[])
{
    fd_set permSet, testSet;
    int fd[MAX_CONNS];              /* Element 0 not used. */
    int i, maxFd = -1;
    char buffer[READ_AMT + 1];
    ssize_t byteCount;

    FD_ZERO (&permSet);
    assert (argc < MAX_CONNS);
    for (i = 1; i < argc; ++i) {
        fd[i] = open (argv[i], O_RDONLY);
        if (fd[i] < 0) {
            fprintf (stderr, "Opening %s failed: %s\n", argv[i],
                    strerror (errno));
```

```
            exit (1);
        } else {
            printf ("Opened %s successfully\n", argv[i]);
        }
        FD_SET (fd[i], &permSet);

        /*
         * Must keep track of the highest fd that is set, it must be passed in as
         * the first argument to select().
         */
        if (fd[i] > maxFd) {
            maxFd = fd[i];
        }
    }
    /*
     * Files opened. "permSet" is now the set of files we care about, and
     * "fd[]" contains the file descriptors to check for each file name.
     */
    for (;;) {

        /*
         * Copy perm set because select() modifies its fd set inputs. If we
         * just passed it in, then we would destroy our original fd set.
         */
        testSet = permSet;

        i = select (maxFd + 1, &testSet, NULL, NULL, NULL);
        assert (i > 0);

        for (i = 1; i < argc; ++i) {
            if (FD_ISSET (fd[i], &testSet)) {
                byteCount = read (fd[i], buffer, READ_AMT);
                assert (byteCount > 0);

                /* Make sure the buffer ends with a null byte for printf's sake. */
                buffer[byteCount] = '\0';
                printf ("Got data from %s: %s", argv[i], buffer);
            }
        }
    }
}
```

lab1_epoll.c

```
/* Copyright 2009, J Cooperstein coop@coopj.com (GPLv2) */

#include <stdio.h>
#include <unistd.h>
#include <fcntl.h>
#include <string.h>
#include <errno.h>
#include <stdlib.h>
#include <sys/epoll.h>

#define MAX_CONNS 10
```

```c
/* private data structure describing an event */

struct my_data
{
    int fd;
    char *filename;
};

int main (int argc, char *argv[])
{
    int fd, epfd, nfd, nev, rfd, maxbytes, maxevents, rc, i, timeout = -1;
    char *buffer, *filename;
    struct epoll_event ep_event[MAX_CONNS], *ep;
    ssize_t nbytes;
    struct my_data *tptr;

    if (argc < 2 || argc >= MAX_CONNS) {
        fprintf (stderr,
                "give at least one filename and not more than %d names\n",
                MAX_CONNS);
        exit (-1);
    }

    nfd = argc - 1;
    maxevents = 4 * nfd;
    maxbytes = getpagesize () - 1;
    buffer = malloc (maxbytes + 1);

    epfd = epoll_create (nfd);
    printf ("epfd from epoll_create = %d\n", epfd);

    /* open all the files and associate data structures with them */

    for (i = 0; i < nfd; i++) {

        filename = argv[i + 1];
        if ((fd = open (filename, O_RDONLY)) < 0) {
            fprintf (stderr, "Opening %s failed: %s\n", filename,
                    strerror (errno));
            exit (1);
        }
        printf ("Opened %s successfully\n", filename);

        tptr = malloc (sizeof (struct my_data));
        tptr->fd = fd;
        tptr->filename = filename;
        ep_event[i].data.ptr = tptr;
        ep_event[i].events = EPOLLIN;

        rc = epoll_ctl (epfd, EPOLL_CTL_ADD, fd, &ep_event[i]);
        printf ("rc from epoll_ctl = %d, for i=%d\n", rc, i);
        printf ("fd = %d for filename = %s\n\n", fd, filename);
    }
```

```
    /* go into a loop and wait on events */

    for (;;) {

        nev = epoll_wait (epfd, ep_event, maxevents, timeout);
        printf ("nev from epoll_wait = %d\n", nev);

        /* found at least one, loop on each and read the data */

        for (i = 0; i < nev; i++) {

            ep = &ep_event[i];

            if (ep->events && EPOLLIN) {
                tptr = ep->data.ptr;
                rfd = tptr->fd;
                filename = tptr->filename;

                nbytes = read (rfd, buffer, maxbytes);
                if (nbytes <= 0) {
                    printf (" Reached end of data, terminating\n");
                    exit (-1);
                }

                /* Make sure the buffer ends with a null byte for printf's sake. */
                buffer[nbytes] = '\0';
                printf ("\nGot data:%2d:%20s: %s\n\n", rfd, filename, buffer);
            }
        }
    }
}
```

28.2   Lab 2: Concurrent Servers

- Take your code for a simple Internet **TCP** server, and adapt it to handle multiple simultaneous connections using select().

- Set a maximum number of simultaneous connections to permit.,

- Make sure you examine the listening socket descriptor so you can accept new connections, as well as listen for incoming data on existing connections.

- To test the server, adapt your simple Internet **TCP** client to open multiple sockets, and then send data to them in random order. You can do this with something like:

```
srand(seed);
....
sd_to_writeto = rand()%number_of_connections;
```

- What happens if you try to open more connections than your server will permit?

- Implement the server using:

  - select().

      – poll().

      – The **epoll** set of functions.

      – fork().

          * You'll need to create a child for each new incoming connection.

          * You'll have to be careful to reap children when they terminate. Otherwise they will become **zombies** and you will be limited in the number of connections you can open.

          * To do this you'll most likely want to use some combination of waitpid() and installing a signal handling routine for SIGCHLD.

      – The **pthread** library.

          * Create multiple threads, using pthread_create() to create a light weight process, or thread, for each new incoming connection.

          * Make sure you **detach** the thread when you create it, either by using pthread_detach() or setting the attributes with pthread_attr_init(), pthread_attr_setdetachstate(). Alternatively, you can wait for the thread to complete with pthread_join().

          * Be careful about any global variables that can be affected in multiple threads, using pthread_mutex_lock() when necessary.

          * Make sure you compile with -pthread.

- To compare results you may wish to insert some timing functions in the client program. If you do, start the timers when all clients have been opened, and stop them before they close, as otherwise you'll just be timing how long it takes to open and close the connections, which is a different metric.

- Fill out the following table with your timing results. You might try 1000 connections with 10000 random client accesses.

Table 28.1: **Concurrent server results**

Method	Time
select	
poll	
fork	
pthread	
epoll	

- **Warning:** You may run into trouble with exceeding your limits on open file descriptors, and maximum memory use. These can be modified with the **ulimit** command (although only **root** can increase the limits.) Memory usage can be cut by limiting stack size.

lab2_client_testscript.sh

```
#!/bin/bash

# Copyright 3/2006, J Cooperstein, coop@coopj.com, (GPLv2)
```

```
HOST="localhost"


NCONS=500
NWRITES=2000

NCONS=1500
NWRITES=2000

# testing values to make sure script ok; above ones more useful
NCONS=100
NWRITES=200



#ulimit -n $(( $NCONS + 16))   # makes ure they are enough open filedesciptors
#                              # must be root if > 1024
#echo The number of file descriptors per process set to: $(ulimit -n)

NLOOP=2

[ -f ./lab1_client ] && LABNO=1
[ -f ./lab2_client ] && LABNO=2


CLIENT=./lab$LABNO\_client

# Any crap left from previous?

echo Cleaning up any previous incarnations .....
for SERVER in \
    ./lab$LABNO\_server_epoll \
    ./lab$LABNO\_server_fork \
    ./lab$LABNO\_server_pthread \
    ./lab$LABNO\_server_select \
    ./lab$LABNO\_server_poll \
    ; do killall -w $SERVER ;
done

for SERVER in \
    ./lab$LABNO\_server_epoll \
    ./lab$LABNO\_server_fork \
    ./lab$LABNO\_server_pthread \
    ./lab$LABNO\_server_select \
    ./lab$LABNO\_server_poll \
    ; do
  echo ""
  echo ======================================================================

  j=1
    while [ $j -le $NLOOP ] ; do
        echo ""
        echo "              RUN $j  of CLIENT=$CLIENT with SERVER=$SERVER "
        $SERVER $NCONS> /dev/null &
# give it a couple of seconds to set up before running client
        sleep 2
```

```
        $CLIENT $HOST $NCONS $NWRITES > /dev/null
        killall -w $SERVER
        j=$(( $j + 1 ))
    done

done

echo ======================================================================
```

lab2_client.c

```c
/* Copyright 2009, J Cooperstein coop@coopj.com (GPLv2) */

#include <stdio.h>
#include <stdlib.h>
#include <errno.h>
#include <string.h>
#include <unistd.h>
#include <sys/socket.h>
#include <netinet/in.h>
#include <netdb.h>
#include <time.h>
#include <sys/time.h>
#include <sys/resource.h>

#define PORTNUM 7177
#define MAX_NUM_CONNECTIONS 10000
#define MSG_MAXSIZE 1024
#define MAX_NWRITES 10

#define DEATH(mess) { perror(mess); exit(errno); };

#define GET_ELAPSED_TIME(tv1,tv2) ( \
  (double)( (tv2.tv_sec - tv1.tv_sec) \
          + .000001 * (tv2.tv_usec - tv1.tv_usec)))

int ncons = 3, *sdvec;
char message[MSG_MAXSIZE], hostname[128];
int nwrites = MAX_NWRITES;

double open_sockets (struct sockaddr_in s_addr)
{
    int j;
    struct timeval tv1, tv2;
    gettimeofday (&tv1, NULL);
    for (j = 0; j < ncons; j++) {
        if ((sdvec[j] = socket (PF_INET, SOCK_STREAM, 0)) < 0)
            DEATH ("socket");
        if (connect (sdvec[j], (struct sockaddr *)&s_addr,
                    sizeof (struct sockaddr_in)) == -1)
            DEATH ("connect");
```

```
            /* put in a short sleep so accept is not overwhelmed */
            usleep (1000);          /* 1 microsecond */
    }
    gettimeofday (&tv2, NULL);
    return GET_ELAPSED_TIME (tv1, tv2);
}

double write_random_sockets (void)
{
    int j, k, count;
    struct timeval tv1, tv2;

    srand (getpid ());              /* initialize random number generator */

    gettimeofday (&tv1, NULL);

    for (k = 0; k < nwrites; k++) {

        /* pick the socket descriptor at random */

        j = rand () % ncons;

        sprintf (message, "Hi. I'm PID %d, socket %3d (k=%3d), on %s\n",
                getpid (), sdvec[j], k, hostname);

        send (sdvec[j], message, strlen (message), 0);

        /* read and display the response */
        count = recv (sdvec[j], message, MSG_MAXSIZE, 0);
        /*
           printf ("socket descriptor %d: ", sdvec[j]);
           fflush (stdout);
           write (STDOUT_FILENO, message, count);
         */
    }
    gettimeofday (&tv2, NULL);

    return GET_ELAPSED_TIME (tv1, tv2);
}

double close_sockets (void)
{
    int j;
    struct timeval tv1, tv2;
    gettimeofday (&tv1, NULL);
    for (j = 0; j < ncons; j++)
        close (sdvec[j]);
    gettimeofday (&tv2, NULL);
    return GET_ELAPSED_TIME (tv1, tv2);
}

int main (int argc, char *argv[])
{
    double open_time, write_time, close_time, elapsed_time;
```

```
struct sockaddr_in s_addr;
struct hostent *s_hostent = NULL;
struct rlimit rlp;

if (argc < 2)
    DEATH ("USAGE: client [hostname|ip_address] #connections #writes\n");

if (argc > 2)
    ncons = atoi (argv[2]);
if (ncons > MAX_NUM_CONNECTIONS)
    ncons = MAX_NUM_CONNECTIONS;
if (argc > 3)
    nwrites = atoi (argv[3]);

/* increase maximum number of file descriptors, must be root! */
rlp.rlim_cur = rlp.rlim_max = ncons + 8;

if (setrlimit (RLIMIT_NOFILE, &rlp) < 0)
    DEATH
        (" Failed to set maxinum number of file descriptors, run as root\n");

gethostname (hostname, 128);

printf
    ("On %s, opening %d connections to %s with  "
     "%d writes randomly distributed\n", hostname, ncons, argv[1], nwrites);

/* determine the server's address */

memset (&s_addr, 0, sizeof (struct sockaddr_in));
s_addr.sin_family = AF_INET;
s_addr.sin_port = htons (PORTNUM);

if (!(s_hostent = gethostbyname (argv[1])))
    DEATH ("gethostbyname");

memcpy (&s_addr.sin_addr, s_hostent->h_addr, s_hostent->h_length);

/* open multiple  internet tcp stream socket */

sdvec = malloc (ncons * sizeof (int));
open_time = open_sockets (s_addr);

fprintf (stderr, "Opened   %6d connections in %12f seconds,"
         "  now going to fire %d writes\n", ncons, open_time, nwrites);

write_time = write_random_sockets ();

fprintf (stderr, "Finished %6d writes      in %12f seconds\n", nwrites,
         write_time);

close_time = close_sockets ();
fprintf (stderr, "Closed   %6d sockets      in %12f seconds\n", ncons,
         close_time);
free (sdvec);
```

```
    elapsed_time = open_time + write_time + close_time;
    fprintf (stderr, "                    TOTALS: %12f %12f %12f %12f\n",
             open_time, write_time, close_time, elapsed_time);

    exit (EXIT_SUCCESS);
}
```

lab2_server_select.c

```
/* Copyright 2009, J Cooperstein coop@coopj.com (GPLv2) */

#include "lab_server.h"

fd_set fdset, testset;
int fdmax = 0;
int nopen = 0;
int *isopen, *cd;
int ncons = MAX_NUM_CONNECTIONS;    /* note this may be modified */

void terminate_client (int ci)
{
    close (cd[ci]);
    isopen[ci] = 0;
    FD_CLR (cd[ci], &fdset);
    nopen--;
    printf ("connection closed   (cd[%2d] = %2d), nopen = %2d\n",
            ci, cd[ci], nopen);
    if (cd[ci] == fdmax)        /* has to be reset */
        fdmax = get_max_fd (fdmax, isopen, cd, ncons);
}

int main (int argc, char *argv[])
{
    int sd, ci, n, backlog = MAX_BACKLOG;
    short port = PORTNUM;

    if (argc > 1)
        ncons = atoi (argv[1]);
    if (ncons > FD_SETSIZE)
        DEATH ("Can't have more than 1024 for select(), and ulimit -s"
               "  must be a bit larger")

            cd = malloc (ncons * sizeof (int));
    isopen = malloc (ncons * sizeof (int));
    gethostname (hostname, 128);

    /* open an internet tcp stream socket */
    /* socket, setsockopt for reuse, bind, listen; */

    sd = get_socket (port, backlog);

    for (ci = 0; ci < ncons; ci++)
        isopen[ci] = 0;
```

```
    FD_ZERO (&fdset);
    FD_SET (sd, &fdset);

    for (;;) {

        /* wait for something to happen on one of the descriptors */

        testset = fdset;
        if (sd > fdmax)
            fdmax = sd;          /* to begin with */
        n = select (fdmax + 1, &testset, NULL, NULL, NULL);

        if (n < 0)
            DEATH ("select");

        /* if you do a time out you have to deal with n = 0 */

        /* accept new connection only if less than the maximum is there */

        if (FD_ISSET (sd, &testset) && (nopen < ncons)) {

            /*  find the first open one */

            ci = accept_one (sd, isopen, cd, ncons);
            isopen[ci] = 1;
            FD_SET (cd[ci], &fdset);
            nopen++;
            if (cd[ci] > fdmax)
                fdmax = cd[ci];
            printf
                ("connection accepted (cd[%2d] = %2d), nopen = %2d\n",
                 ci, cd[ci], nopen);

        }
        /* service existing connections */

        for (ci = 0; ci < ncons; ci++) {
            if (isopen[ci] && FD_ISSET (cd[ci], &testset))
                if (handle_client (cd[ci]))
                    terminate_client (ci);
        }
    }

    close (sd);
    free (cd);
    free (isopen);
    exit (EXIT_SUCCESS);
}
```

lab2_server_poll.c

```
 /* Copyright 2009, J Cooperstein coop@coopj.com (GPLv2) */

#include <sys/poll.h>
#include "lab_server.h"
```

```
struct pollfd *ufds;
int fdmax = 0;
int nopen = 0;
int *isopen, *cd;
int ncons = MAX_NUM_CONNECTIONS;      /* note this may be modified */

void terminate_client (int ci)
{
    struct pollfd *pfd = &ufds[ci];
    close (cd[ci]);
    isopen[ci] = 0;
    pfd->fd = -1;
    pfd->events = 0;
    nopen--;
    printf ("connection closed   (cd[%2d] = %2d), nopen = %2d\n",
            ci, cd[ci], nopen);
    if (cd[ci] == fdmax)         /* has to be reset */
        fdmax = get_max_fd (fdmax, isopen, cd, ncons);
}
int main (int argc, char *argv[])
{
    int sd, ci, n, backlog = MAX_BACKLOG, timeout = -1, nfds, nconsp1;
    short port = PORTNUM;
    struct pollfd *pfd, *pfd0;

    if (argc > 1)
        ncons = atoi (argv[1]);
    nconsp1 = ncons + 1;

    cd = malloc ((nconsp1 + 8) * sizeof (int));
    isopen = malloc ((nconsp1 + 8) * sizeof (int));
    ufds = malloc ((nconsp1 + 8) * sizeof (struct pollfd));
    memset (ufds, 0, (nconsp1 + 8) * sizeof (struct pollfd));

    /* increase maximum number of file descriptors, must be root! */

    /* a few extra, for 0, 1, 2 etc. */
    check_and_set_max_fd (nconsp1 + 8);

    gethostname (hostname, 128);

    /* open an internet tcp stream socket */
    /* socket, setsockopt for reuse, bind, listen; */
    sd = get_socket (port, backlog);

    /* for the listening socket */

    pfd0 = &ufds[0];
    pfd0->fd = sd;
    pfd0->events = POLLIN;

    isopen[0] = 0;

    for (ci = 1; ci < nconsp1 + 8; ci++) {
```

```
        pfd = &ufds[ci];
        pfd->fd = -1;
        pfd->events = 0;
        isopen[ci] = 0;
    }

    for (;;) {

        /* wait for something to happen on one of the descriptors */

        nfds = 1 + nopen;
        if (sd > fdmax)
            fdmax = sd;          /* to begin with */

        /*        n = poll (ufds, nconsp1, timeout);   */
        n = poll (&ufds[0], fdmax + 1, timeout);

        if (n < 0)
            DEATH ("poll");

        /* if you do a time out you have to deal with n = 0 */

        /* accept new connection only if less than the maximum is there */

        if ((pfd0->revents && POLLIN) && (nopen < ncons)) {
            isopen[0] = 1;

            /*  find the first open one */

            ci = accept_one (sd, isopen, cd, ncons);
            isopen[ci] = 1;
            pfd = &ufds[ci];
            pfd->fd = cd[ci];
            pfd->events = POLLIN;
            nopen++;
            if (cd[ci] > fdmax)
                fdmax = cd[ci];
            printf
                ("connection accepted (cd[%2d] = %2d), nopen = %2d\n",
                 ci, cd[ci], nopen);

        }
        /* service existing connections */

        for (ci = 1; ci < nconsp1; ci++) {
            pfd = &ufds[ci];
            if (isopen[ci] && (pfd->revents && POLLIN)) {
                if (handle_client (cd[ci]))
                    terminate_client (ci);
            }
            fflush (stdout);
        }
    }
    close (sd);
    free (cd);
```

```
        free (isopen);
        exit (EXIT_SUCCESS);
}
```

lab2_server_epoll.c

```
 /* Copyright 2009, J Cooperstein coop@coopj.com (GPLv2) */

#include <sys/epoll.h>
#include "lab_server.h"

/* private data structure describing an event */

int nopen = 0;
int *isopen, *cd;
int ncons = MAX_NUM_CONNECTIONS;       /* note this may be modified */
struct my_data
{
    int fd;
};
struct epoll_event *ep_event, *ep, *ep_sd;

void terminate_client (int sdes, int i)
{
    int ci;
    struct epoll_event *ept;
    for (ci = 0; ci < ncons; ci++) {
        if (sdes == cd[ci]) {
            close (sdes);
            isopen[ci] = 0;
            nopen--;
            ept = &ep_event[i];
            free (ept->data.ptr);
            break;
        }
    }
    printf ("connection closed   (cd[%2d] = %2d), nopen = %2d\n",
            ci, cd[ci], nopen);
}

void accept_it (int sd, int epfd)
{
    int ci;
    struct my_data *tptr;
    struct epoll_event *ept;

    /*  find the first open one */

    ci = accept_one (sd, isopen, cd, ncons);
    isopen[ci] = 1;

    tptr = malloc (sizeof (struct my_data));
    tptr->fd = cd[ci];
    ept = &ep_event[ci];
    ept->data.ptr = tptr;
```

```
        ept->events = EPOLLIN;
        epoll_ctl (epfd, EPOLL_CTL_ADD, cd[ci], ept);
        nopen++;
        printf
            ("connection accepted (cd[%2d] = %2d), nopen = %2d\n",
             ci, cd[ci], nopen);
}

int main (int argc, char *argv[])
{
        short port = PORTNUM;
        int sd, ci, n, i, epfd, backlog = MAX_BACKLOG, timeout = -1;
        int maxevents = 100;        /* no need to be large */
        struct my_data *tptr;

        if (argc > 1)
            ncons = atoi (argv[1]);

        cd = malloc ((ncons + 8) * sizeof (int));
        isopen = malloc ((ncons + 8) * sizeof (int));
        ep_event = malloc ((ncons + 8) * sizeof (struct epoll_event));
        memset (ep_event, 0, (ncons + 8) * sizeof (struct epoll_event));
        for (ci = 0; ci < ncons + 8; ci++)
            isopen[ci] = 0;

        /* a few extra, for 0, 1, 2 etc. */
        check_and_set_max_fd (ncons + 8);

        gethostname (hostname, 128);

        /* open an internet tcp stream socket */
        /* socket, setsockopt for reuse, bind, listen; */
        sd = get_socket (port, backlog);

        /* set up epoll */
        epfd = epoll_create (ncons);

        /* for the listening socket */

        tptr = malloc (sizeof (struct my_data));
        tptr->fd = sd;
        ep_sd = malloc (sizeof (struct epoll_event));
        ep_sd->data.ptr = tptr;
        ep_sd->events = EPOLLIN;

        epoll_ctl (epfd, EPOLL_CTL_ADD, sd, ep_sd);

        for (;;) {

            /* wait for something to happen on one of the descriptors */
            maxevents = 2;

            n = epoll_wait (epfd, ep_event, maxevents, timeout);

            if (n < 0)
```

```
            DEATH ("epoll");

        /* if you do a time out you have to deal with n = 0 */

        for (i = 0; i < n; i++) {

            ep = &ep_event[i];
            tptr = ep->data.ptr;

            /* accept new connection only if less than the maximum is there */

            if (tptr->fd == sd) {
                if (nopen < ncons)
                    accept_it (sd, epfd);
            } else {

                /* service existing connections */
                /* note arg is actual descriptor */
                if (handle_client (tptr->fd))
                    terminate_client (tptr->fd, i);
            }
        }
    }
    free (cd);
    free (isopen);
    close (epfd);
    close (sd);
    exit (EXIT_SUCCESS);
}
```

lab2_server_fork.c

```
 /* Copyright 2009, J Cooperstein coop@coopj.com (GPLv2) */

#include <signal.h>
#include <sys/wait.h>

#include "lab_server.h"

#define STACK_SIZE 64              /* in KB */
int nopen = 0;
pid_t *pid;
int *isopen, *cd;
int ncons = MAX_NUM_CONNECTIONS;    /* note this may be modified */

void terminate_client (int ci)
{
    close (cd[ci]);
    printf ("connection closed for pid=%d  (cd[%2d] = %2d)\n",
            getpid (), ci, cd[ci]);
    fflush (stdout);
    exit (EXIT_SUCCESS);
}

void cleanupkids (int sig)
```

```c
{
    pid_t pid_test;
    int ci, status;

    for (ci = 0; ci < ncons; ci++) {

        if (!isopen[ci])
            continue;

        pid_test = waitpid (pid[ci], &status, WNOHANG);

        if (pid_test <= 0)       /* this guy is not done */
            continue;

        /* this guy is finished */
        isopen[ci] = 0;
        nopen--;
        printf ("caught the kid pid=%d (cd[%2d] = %2d), nopen = %2d\n",
                pid_test, ci, cd[ci], nopen);
        fflush (stdout);
        close (cd[ci]);
    }
}

int main (int argc, char *argv[])
{
    int sd, ci, backlog = MAX_BACKLOG;
    short port = PORTNUM;

    if (argc > 1)
        ncons = atoi (argv[1]);

    /* decrease stack size, non-privilged operation */
    /*    shrink_stack (STACK_SIZE); not needed for parent */

    /* increase maximum number of file descriptors, must be root! */
    /* a few extra, for 0, 1, 2 etc. */
    check_and_set_max_fd (ncons + 8);

    cd = malloc (ncons * sizeof (int));
    isopen = malloc (ncons * sizeof (int));
    pid = malloc (ncons * sizeof (pid_t));
    gethostname (hostname, 128);

    signal (SIGCHLD, cleanupkids);

    /* open an internet tcp stream socket */
    /* socket, setsockopt for reuse, bind, listen; */

    sd = get_socket (port, backlog);

    for (ci = 0; ci < ncons; ci++)
        isopen[ci] = 0;

    for (;;) {
```

```
        /* accept new connection only if less than
            the maximum is there */
        while (nopen == ncons) {
            /* reap any children; there may be a
                race condition or signal pileup! */
            cleanupkids (SIGCHLD);
        }

        /*  find the first open one */

        ci = accept_one (sd, isopen, cd, ncons);
        isopen[ci] = 1;
        nopen++;
        printf ("connection accepted (cd[%2d] = %2d), nopen = %2d\n",
                ci, cd[ci], nopen);
        fflush (stdout);

        /* fork off a child to handle the connection */

        pid[ci] = fork ();
        if (pid[ci] < 0)
            DEATH ("Forking");

        if (pid[ci] == 0) {       /* child */

            /* decrease stack size, non-privilged operation */
            shrink_stack (STACK_SIZE);
            /* can set back for kids */
            set_max_fd (16);

            while (!handle_client (cd[ci])) ;
            terminate_client (ci);
        } else {                   /* parent */
            printf (" I forked for ci=%d, pid=%d\n", ci, pid[ci]);
            fflush (stdout);
        }
    }

    close (sd);
    free (isopen);
    free (cd);
    exit (EXIT_SUCCESS);
}
```

lab2_server_pthread.c

```
/* Copyright 2009, J Cooperstein coop@coopj.com (GPLv2) */

#include "lab_server.h"

#include <pthread.h>

#define STACK_SIZE 128          /* in KB */
```

```
pthread_t *thread_id;
int *thread_data;
pthread_mutex_t nopen_lock = PTHREAD_MUTEX_INITIALIZER;
volatile int nopen = 0;           /* note the volatile ! */
int *isopen, *cd;
int ncons = MAX_NUM_CONNECTIONS;     /* note this may be modified */

void terminate_client (int ci)
{
    isopen[ci] = 0;
    pthread_mutex_lock (&nopen_lock);
    nopen--;
    close (cd[ci]);
    /* this guy is finished */
    printf ("connection closed    (cd[%2d] = %2d), nopen = %2d\n",
            ci, cd[ci], nopen);
    pthread_mutex_unlock (&nopen_lock);

    fflush (stdout);
}
void *handle_clientp (void *arg)
{
    int *j, ci;
    j = arg;
    ci = *j;
    while (!handle_client (cd[ci])) ;
    terminate_client (ci);
    return NULL;
}

int main (int argc, char *argv[])
{
    int rc, sd, ci, backlog = MAX_BACKLOG;
    short port = PORTNUM;
    pthread_attr_t thread_attr;

    if (argc > 1)
        ncons = atoi (argv[1]);

    /* decrease stack size, non-privilged operation */

    rc = pthread_attr_init (&thread_attr);
    rc = pthread_attr_setstacksize (&thread_attr, STACK_SIZE * 1024);

    /*  could do this instead of through pthread library */
    /*    shrink_stack (STACK_SIZE); */

    /* increase maximum number of file descriptors, must be root! */
    /* a few extra, for 0, 1, 2 etc. */
    check_and_set_max_fd (ncons + 8);

    cd = malloc (ncons * sizeof (int));
    isopen = malloc (ncons * sizeof (int));

    thread_id = malloc (ncons * sizeof (pthread_t));
```

```
    thread_data = malloc (ncons * sizeof (int));

    gethostname (hostname, 128);

    /* open an internet tcp stream socket */
    /* socket, setsockopt for reuse, bind, listen; */

    sd = get_socket (port, backlog);

    for (ci = 0; ci < ncons; ci++)
        isopen[ci] = 0;

    for (;;) {

        /* accept new connection only if less than the maximum is there */
        while (nopen == ncons) {
            /* wait for a thread to complete */
        }

        /*  find the first open one */

        ci = accept_one (sd, isopen, cd, ncons);
        isopen[ci] = 1;
        pthread_mutex_lock (&nopen_lock);
        nopen++;
        printf ("connection accepted (cd[%2d] = %2d), nopen = %2d\n",
                ci, cd[ci], nopen);
        pthread_mutex_unlock (&nopen_lock);
        fflush (stdout);

        /* spin off a new thread to handle the connection */
        thread_data[ci] = ci;

        if (pthread_create
            (thread_id + ci, &thread_attr, handle_clientp, thread_data + ci))
            DEATH ("Thread Creation");

        if (pthread_detach (thread_id[ci]))
            DEATH ("Thread Detaching");

        printf (" For ci=%d, new thread_pid=%ld\n", ci, thread_id[ci]);
        fflush (stdout);
    }

    free (isopen);
    free (cd);
    close (sd);
    exit (EXIT_SUCCESS);
}
```

Chapter 29

Inter Process Communication

29.1 Lab 1: Examining System V IPC Activity

- To get an overall summary of **System V IPC** activity on your system, do:

```
$ ipcs
------ Shared Memory Segments --------
key        shmid     owner    perms    bytes      nattch    status
0x00000000 0         root     777      135168     1
0x00000000 393217    coop     600      393216     2         dest
0x00000000 425986    coop     600      393216     2         dest
0x00000000 262147    coop     600      393216     2         dest
0x00000000 294916    coop     600      393216     2         dest
0x00000000 327685    coop     600      393216     2         dest
0x00000000 360454    coop     600      393216     2         dest
0x00000000 458759    coop     600      393216     2         dest
0x00000000 491528    coop     600      393216     2         dest
0x00000000 524297    coop     600      393216     2         dest
0x00000000 557066    coop     600      393216     2         dest
0x00000000 819211    coop     600      393216     2         dest
0x00000000 622604    coop     600      393216     2         dest
0x00000000 655373    coop     600      393216     2         dest
```

```
0x00000000 3833870    coop     600      393216     2         dest
0x00000000 753679     coop     600      393216     2         dest
0x00000000 786448     coop     600      393216     2         dest
0x00000000 950289     coop     600      12288      2         dest
0x00000000 983058     coop     600      393216     2         dest
0x00000000 1015827    coop     600      12288      2         dest
0x00000000 3866644    coop     600      393216     2         dest
0x00000000 3407893    root     644      790528     2         dest
0x00000000 3440662    root     644      790528     2         dest
0x00000000 3473431    root     644      790528     2         dest


------ Semaphore Arrays --------
key        semid     owner     perms    nsems


------ Message Queues --------
key        msqid     owner     perms    used-bytes  messages
```

Note that the currently running shared memory segments all have a key of 0 which means IPC_PRIVATE, and all but one are marked for destruction when there are no further attachments. Later when you are doing exercises you should repeat this command to see the results.

- One can gain further information about the processes that have created the segments and last attached to them with:

```
$ ipcs -p

------ Shared Memory Creator/Last-op --------
shmid        owner      cpid      lpid
0            root       3867      31573
393217       coop       4076      19499
425986       coop       4074      3867
262147       coop       4076      19499
294916       coop       4703      3867
327685       coop       4705      3867
360454       coop       4074      3867
458759       coop       4383      5516
491528       coop       4070      3867
524297       coop       4070      3867
557066       coop       4738      3867
819211       coop       5012      3867
622604       coop       4835      3867
655373       coop       4837      3867
3833870      coop       21958     3867
753679       coop       4987      4466
786448       coop       5012      3867
950289       coop       4070      3867
983058       coop       4703      3867
1015827      coop       4703      3867
3866644      coop       21958     3867
3407893      root       3867      17031
3440662      root       3867      17031
3473431      root       3867      17031


------ Message Queues PIDs --------
msqid        owner      lspid     lrpid
```

so by doing:

```
$ ps ax | grep -e 3867 -e 5012

  3867 tty7      Ss+     1:30 /usr/bin/Xorg :0 -br -audit 0 -auth /var/gdm/:0.Xauth -nolisten tcp
  5012 ?         Sl      0:20 /usr/lib64/thunderbird-2.0.0.22/thunderbird-bin
 22162 pts/0     S+      0:00 grep -e 3867 -e 5012
```

we see **thunderbird** is using a shared memory segment created by the **X** server.

- Do this on your system and identify the various resources being used and by who. Are there any potential leaks on the system?

Chapter 30

Shared Memory

30.1   Lab 1: Shared Memory

- Construct one or more programs to pass messages to each other in shared memory.

- The receiving program may terminate when it receives the message from the sending program.

- Make sure the shared memory is released when no longer needed.

- You may write more than one program, or write one program that can do multiple actions based on the arguments.

- Two solutions are given; one for System V IPC and one for POSIX IPC.

- The solutions are written so that they take an argument, which can be either `create`, `remove`, `send`, or `receive`, which controls their action.

- Don't forget to compile with `-lrt` for the POSIX IPC solution.

`lab1_v_shm.c`

```c
/* Copyright 2009, J Cooperstein coop@coopj.com (GPLv2) */
#include <unistd.h>
#include <stdlib.h>
#include <stdio.h>
#include <sys/types.h>
#include <sys/ipc.h>
#include <sys/shm.h>
#include <errno.h>
#include <string.h>

#define DEATH(mess) { perror(mess); exit(errno); }

#define KEY (key_t)26
#define SIZE 8196

void create_it (void)
{
    int shmid;
    void *shm_area;

    if ((shmid = shmget (KEY, SIZE, IPC_CREAT | 0666)) == -1)
        DEATH ("shmget");

    if ((shm_area = shmat (shmid, (void *)0, 0)) == (void *)-1)
        DEATH ("shmat");

    printf ("CREATE: Memory attached at %lX\n", (unsigned long)shm_area);

    if (shmdt (shm_area) == -1)
        DEATH ("shmdt");

    printf ("Shared Memory Region successfully created\n");

    exit (EXIT_SUCCESS);
}

void remove_it (void)
{
    int shmid;

    if ((shmid = shmget (KEY, SIZE, 0)) == -1)
        DEATH ("shmget");

    if (shmctl (shmid, IPC_RMID, 0))
        DEATH ("shmctl");

    printf ("Marked shared memory segment for deletion\n");

    exit (EXIT_SUCCESS);
}

void send_it (void)
{
    int shmid, iflag = 1;
    void *shm_area;
```

```c
    if ((shmid = shmget (KEY, SIZE, 0)) == -1)
        DEATH ("shmget");

    if ((shm_area = shmat (shmid, (void *)0, 0)) == (void *)-1)
        DEATH ("shmat");

    printf ("SEND: Memory attached at %lX\n", (unsigned long)shm_area);
    memcpy (shm_area, &iflag, 4);

    if (shmdt (shm_area) == -1)
        DEATH ("shmdt");

    printf ("SENDND has successfully completed\n");

    exit (EXIT_SUCCESS);
}

void receive_it (void)
{
    int shmid, iflag = 8;
    void *shm_area;

    if ((shmid = shmget (KEY, SIZE, 0)) == -1)
        DEATH ("shmget");

    if ((shm_area = shmat (shmid, (void *)0, 0)) == (void *)-1)
        DEATH ("shmat");

    printf ("RCV: Memory attached at %lX\n", (unsigned long)shm_area);
    memcpy (shm_area, &iflag, 4);

    printf ("iflag is now = %d\n", iflag);
    while (iflag == 8) {
        memcpy (&iflag, shm_area, 4);
        sleep (1);
    }
    printf ("RCV has successfully completed\n");
    printf ("iflag is now = %d\n", iflag);

    if (shmdt (shm_area) == -1)
        DEATH ("shmdt");

    exit (EXIT_SUCCESS);
}

int main (int argc, char *argv[])
{
    if (argc > 1) {
        if (!strcasecmp ("create", argv[1]))
            create_it ();
        if (!strcasecmp ("remove", argv[1]))
            remove_it ();
        if (!strcasecmp ("receive", argv[1]))
            receive_it ();
```

```
        if (!strcasecmp ("send", argv[1]))
            send_it ();
    }
    printf ("Usage: %s  create | remove | receive | send \n", argv[0]);
    exit (-1);
}
```

lab1_p_shm.c

```
 /* Copyright 2009, J Cooperstein coop@coopj.com (GPLv2) */
#include <unistd.h>
#include <stdlib.h>
#include <stdio.h>
#include <errno.h>
#include <string.h>
#include <fcntl.h>
#include <sys/mman.h>
#include <sys/types.h>

#define DEATH(mess) { perror(mess); exit(errno); }
#define SIZE 8196
#define NAME "/my_shm"

void create_it (void)
{
    int shm_fd;

    if ((shm_fd = shm_open (NAME, O_RDWR | O_CREAT | O_EXCL, 0666)) == -1)
        DEATH ("shm_open");

    ftruncate (shm_fd, SIZE);

    printf ("Shared Memory Region successfully created\n");

    exit (EXIT_SUCCESS);
}

void remove_it (void)
{
    int shm_fd;

    if ((shm_fd = shm_open (NAME, O_RDWR, 0) == -1))
        DEATH ("shm_open");

    if (shm_unlink (NAME))
        DEATH ("shm_unlink");

    printf ("Shared Memory Region successfully destroyed\n");

    exit (EXIT_SUCCESS);
}

void send_it (void)
{
    int shm_fd, iflag = 1;
```

```
        void *shm_area;

        if ((shm_fd = shm_open (NAME, O_RDWR, 0)) == -1)
            DEATH ("shm_open");

        shm_area = mmap (NULL, SIZE, PROT_READ | PROT_WRITE, MAP_SHARED, shm_fd, 0);

        if (shm_area == MAP_FAILED)
            DEATH ("mmap");

        printf ("SEND: Memory attached at %lX\n", (unsigned long)shm_area);
        memcpy (shm_area, &iflag, 4);

        if (munmap (shm_area, SIZE))
            DEATH ("munmap");

        printf ("SEND has successfully completed\n");

        exit (EXIT_SUCCESS);
}

void receive_it (void)
{
        int shm_fd, iflag = 8;
        void *shm_area;

        if ((shm_fd = shm_open (NAME, O_RDWR, 0)) == -1)
            DEATH ("shm_open");

        shm_area = mmap (NULL, SIZE, PROT_READ | PROT_WRITE, MAP_SHARED, shm_fd, 0);

        if (shm_area == MAP_FAILED)
            DEATH ("mmap");

        printf ("RCV: Memory attached at %lX\n", (unsigned long)shm_area);

        memcpy (shm_area, &iflag, 4);
        printf ("iflag is now = %d\n", iflag);

        while (iflag == 8) {
            memcpy (&iflag, shm_area, 4);
            sleep (1);
        }
        printf ("RCV has successfully completed\n");
        printf ("iflag is now = %d\n", iflag);

        if (munmap (shm_area, SIZE))
            DEATH ("munmap");

        exit (EXIT_SUCCESS);
}

int main (int argc, char *argv[])
{
        if (argc > 1) {
```

```
        if (!strcasecmp ("create", argv[1]))
            create_it ();
        if (!strcasecmp ("remove", argv[1]))
            remove_it ();
        if (!strcasecmp ("receive", argv[1]))
            receive_it ();
        if (!strcasecmp ("send", argv[1]))
            send_it ();
    }
    printf ("Usage: %s  create | remove | receive | send \n", argv[0]);
    exit (-1);
}
```

Chapter 31

Semaphores

31.1   Lab 1: Semaphores

- Write one or more programs that protect a critical section with a semaphore.

- The critical section can be as simple as a sleep().

- You may write more than one program, or write one program that can do multiple actions based on the arguments.

- Two solutions are given; one for System V IPC and one for POSIX IPC.

- The solutions are written so that they take an argument, which can be either create, remove, or protect, which controls their action.

- Don't forget to compile with -lrt for the POSIX IPC solution.

lab1_v_sem.c

```
/* Copyright 2009, J Cooperstein coop@coopj.com (GPLv2) */
#include <stdio.h>
```

```
#include <sys/types.h>
#include <sys/ipc.h>
#include <sys/sem.h>
#include <errno.h>
#include <unistd.h>
#include <string.h>
#include <stdlib.h>

#define KEY                 (key_t)261
#define DEATH(mess) { perror(mess); exit(errno); }

union semun
{
    int val;                    /* value for SETVAL */
    struct semid_ds *buf;       /* buffer for IPC_STAT, IPC_SET */
    unsigned short int *array;  /* array for GETALL, SETALL */
    struct seminfo *__buf;      /* buffer for IPC_INFO */
};

void set_sem (int semid, int val)
{
    struct sembuf buffer;

    buffer.sem_num = 0;         /* first (and only) semaphore in the list */
    buffer.sem_op = val;        /* either wait (-1) or release (1) */
    buffer.sem_flg = SEM_UNDO;  /* let the system clean up after us */

    if ((semop (semid, &buffer, 1)) == -1)
        DEATH ("setop");
}

void create_it (void)
{
    int semid;
    union semun sem_union;

    printf ("Creating a new semaphore\n");
    if ((semid = semget (KEY, 1, 0666 | IPC_CREAT)) == -1)
        DEATH ("semget");

    printf ("Initializing the semaphore.\n");
    sem_union.val = 1;
    if ((semctl (semid, 0, SETVAL, sem_union)) == -1)
        DEATH ("semctl");

    printf ("Semaphore successfully created and initialized\n");
    exit (EXIT_SUCCESS);
}

void remove_it (void)
{
    int semid;
    union semun sem_union;

    if ((semid = semget (KEY, 1, 0)) == -1)
```

```
            DEATH ("semget");

    if ((semctl (semid, 0, IPC_RMID, sem_union)) == -1)
            DEATH ("semctl");

    printf ("Semaphore successfully deleted\n");
    exit (EXIT_SUCCESS);
}

void protect_it (void)
{
    int semid, i;

    if ((semid = semget (KEY, 1, 0)) == -1)
            DEATH ("semget");

    for (i = 0; i < 4; i++) {
        set_sem (semid, -1);
        printf ("Entering critical section, %d, pid=%d\n", i, getpid ());
        sleep (3);
        printf (" Leaving critical section, %d, pid=%d\n", i, getpid ());
        set_sem (semid, 1);
        sleep (3);
    }
    printf ("PROTECT region exited for pid=%d\n", getpid ());

    exit (EXIT_SUCCESS);
}

int main (int argc, char *argv[])
{
    if (argc > 1) {
        if (!strcasecmp ("create", argv[1]))
            create_it ();
        if (!strcasecmp ("remove", argv[1]))
            remove_it ();
        if (!strcasecmp ("protect", argv[1]))
            protect_it ();
    }
    printf ("Usage: %s  create | remove | protect\n", argv[0]);
    exit (-1);
}
```

lab1_p_sem.c

```
 /* Copyright 2009, J Cooperstein coop@coopj.com (GPLv2) */
#include <stdio.h>
#include <stdlib.h>
#include <pthread.h>
#include <unistd.h>
#include <errno.h>
#include <semaphore.h>
#include <string.h>
#include <fcntl.h>
```

```c
#define DEATH(mess) { perror(mess); exit(errno); }
#define NAME "/my_sem"

void create_it (void)
{
    sem_t *mysem;

    if ((mysem = sem_open (NAME, O_CREAT | O_EXCL, 0666, 1)) == SEM_FAILED)
        DEATH ("sem_open");

    if ((sem_close (mysem)) == -1)
        DEATH ("sem_close");

    printf ("Semaphore successfully created and initialized\n");
    exit (EXIT_SUCCESS);
}

void remove_it (void)
{
    if ((sem_unlink (NAME)) == -1)
        DEATH ("sem_unlink");

    printf ("Semaphore successfully deleted\n");
    exit (EXIT_SUCCESS);
}

void protect_it (void)
{
    int i;
    sem_t *mysem;

    printf ("Attaching to the semaphore\n");

    if ((mysem = sem_open (NAME, 0)) == SEM_FAILED)
        DEATH ("sem_open");

    for (i = 0; i < 4; i++) {
        if (sem_wait (mysem))
            DEATH ("sem_wait");
        printf ("Entering critical section, %d, pid=%d\n", i, getpid ());
        sleep (3);
        printf (" Leaving critical section, %d, pid=%d\n", i, getpid ());
        if (sem_post (mysem))
            DEATH ("sem_post");
        sleep (3);
    }
    printf ("PROTECT region exited for pid=%d\n", getpid ());

    if ((sem_close (mysem)) == -1)
        DEATH ("sem_close");

    exit (EXIT_SUCCESS);
}

int main (int argc, char *argv[])
```

```
{
    if (argc > 1) {
        if (!strcasecmp ("create", argv[1]))
            create_it ();
        if (!strcasecmp ("remove", argv[1]))
            remove_it ();
        if (!strcasecmp ("protect", argv[1]))
            protect_it ();
    }
    printf ("Usage: %s  create | remove | protect\n", argv[0]);
    exit (-1);
}
```

31.2 Lab 2: Semaphores and Shared Memory

- Modify the shared memory lab to use semaphores to have the programs pass messages to each other in shared memory.

- The first program should get some input from the user, stuff it into shared memory, and release the semaphore to signal the second program.

- The second program should read the message and display it, then release the semaphore to let the first one know that he's ready for more.

- You may write more than one program, or write one program that can do multiple actions based on the arguments.

- Two solutions are given; one for System V IPC and one for POSIX IPC.

- The solutions are written so that they take an argument, which can be either `create`, `remove`, `send`, or `receive`, which controls their action.

- Don't forget to compile with `-lrt` for the POSIX IPC solution.

lab2_v_sem_shm.c

```
/* Copyright 2009, J Cooperstein coop@coopj.com (GPLv2) */
#include <unistd.h>
#include <stdlib.h>
#include <stdio.h>
#include <sys/types.h>
#include <sys/ipc.h>
#include <sys/shm.h>
#include <sys/sem.h>
#include <errno.h>
#include <string.h>

#define DEATH(mess) { perror(mess); exit(errno); }

#define KEY (key_t)26
#define SIZE 8196

union semun
```

```
{
    int val;                    /* value for SETVAL */
    struct semid_ds *buf;       /* buffer for IPC_STAT, IPC_SET */
    unsigned short int *array;  /* array for GETALL, SETALL */
    struct seminfo *__buf;      /* buffer for IPC_INFO */
};

void set_sem (int semid, int val)
{
    struct sembuf buffer;

    buffer.sem_num = 0;         /* first (and only) semaphore in the list */
    buffer.sem_op = val;        /* either wait (-1) or release (1) */
    buffer.sem_flg = SEM_UNDO;  /* let the system clean up after us */

    if ((semop (semid, &buffer, 1)) == -1)
        DEATH ("setop");
}

void create_it (void)
{
    int shmid, semid;
    void *shm_area;
    union semun sem_union;

    if ((shmid = shmget (KEY, SIZE, IPC_CREAT | 0666)) == -1)
        DEATH ("shmget");

    if ((shm_area = shmat (shmid, (void *)0, 0)) == (void *)-1)
        DEATH ("shmat");

    printf ("CREATE: Memory attached at %1X\n", (unsigned long)shm_area);

    if (shmdt (shm_area) == -1)
        DEATH ("shmdt");

    if ((semid = semget (KEY, 1, 0666 | IPC_CREAT)) == -1)
        DEATH ("semget");

    sem_union.val = 1;
    if ((semctl (semid, 0, SETVAL, sem_union)) == -1)
        DEATH ("semctl");

    printf ("Semaphore successfully created and initialized\n");

    exit (EXIT_SUCCESS);
}

void remove_it (void)
{
    int shmid, semid;
    union semun sem_union;

    if ((shmid = shmget (KEY, SIZE, 0)) == -1)
        DEATH ("shmget");
```

```
        if (shmctl (shmid, IPC_RMID, 0))
            DEATH ("shmctl");

        printf ("Marked shared memory segment for deletion\n");

        if ((semid = semget (KEY, 1, 0)) == -1)
            DEATH ("semget");

        if ((semctl (semid, 0, IPC_RMID, sem_union)) == -1)
            DEATH ("semctl");

        printf ("Semaphore successfully deleted\n");

        exit (EXIT_SUCCESS);
}

void send_it (void)
{
        int shmid, semid, i;
        void *shm_area;

        if ((shmid = shmget (KEY, SIZE, 0)) == -1)
            DEATH ("shmget");

        if ((shm_area = shmat (shmid, (void *)0, 0)) == (void *)-1)
            DEATH ("shmat");

        printf ("SEND: Memory attached at %lX\n", (unsigned long)shm_area);

        if ((semid = semget (KEY, 1, 0)) == -1)
            DEATH ("semget");

        for (i = 0; i < 4; i++) {
            set_sem (semid, -1);    /* wait */
            printf ("Please type a message:\n");
            fgets (shm_area, SIZE, stdin);
            set_sem (semid, 1);     /* release */
            usleep (1000);          /* pause a millisecond to give other guy a chance */
        }

        if (shmdt (shm_area) == -1)
            DEATH ("shmdt");

        printf ("SENDND has successfully completed\n");

        exit (EXIT_SUCCESS);
}

void receive_it (void)
{
        int shmid, semid, i;
        void *shm_area;

        if ((shmid = shmget (KEY, SIZE, 0)) == -1)
```

```
        DEATH ("shmget");

    if ((shm_area = shmat (shmid, (void *)0, 0)) == (void *)-1)
        DEATH ("shmat");

    printf ("RCV: Memory attached at %1X\n", (unsigned long)shm_area);

    if ((semid = semget (KEY, 1, 0)) == -1)
        DEATH ("semget");

    for (i = 0; i < 4; i++) {
        set_sem (semid, -1);    /* wait */
        fprintf (stdout, "%s\n", (char *)shm_area);
        set_sem (semid, 1);     /* release */
        usleep (1000);          /* pause a millisecond to give other guy a chance */
    }

    printf ("RCV has successfully completed\n");

    if (shmdt (shm_area) == -1)
        DEATH ("shmdt");

    exit (EXIT_SUCCESS);
}

int main (int argc, char *argv[])
{
    if (argc > 1) {
        if (!strcasecmp ("create", argv[1]))
            create_it ();
        if (!strcasecmp ("remove", argv[1]))
            remove_it ();
        if (!strcasecmp ("receive", argv[1]))
            receive_it ();
        if (!strcasecmp ("send", argv[1]))
            send_it ();
    }
    printf ("Usage: %s  create | remove | receive | send \n", argv[0]);
    exit (-1);
}
```

lab2_p_sem_shm.c

```
 /* Copyright 2009, J Cooperstein coop@coopj.com (GPLv2) */
#include <unistd.h>
#include <stdlib.h>
#include <stdio.h>
#include <errno.h>
#include <string.h>
#include <fcntl.h>
#include <semaphore.h>
#include <sys/mman.h>
#include <sys/types.h>

#define DEATH(mess) { perror(mess); exit(errno); }
```

```c
#define SIZE 8196
#define NAME_SHM "/my_shm"
#define NAME_SEM "/my_sem"

void create_it (void)
{
    int shm_fd;
    sem_t *mysem;

    if ((shm_fd = shm_open (NAME_SHM, O_RDWR | O_CREAT | O_EXCL, 0666)) == -1)
        DEATH ("shm_open");

    ftruncate (shm_fd, SIZE);

    printf ("Shared Memory Region successfully created\n");

    if ((mysem = sem_open (NAME_SEM, O_CREAT | O_EXCL, 0666, 1)) == SEM_FAILED)
        DEATH ("sem_open");

    if ((sem_close (mysem)) == -1)
        DEATH ("sem_close");

    printf ("Semaphore successfully created and initialized\n");
    exit (EXIT_SUCCESS);
}

void remove_it (void)
{
    int shm_fd;
    sem_t *mysem;

    if ((shm_fd = shm_open (NAME_SHM, O_RDWR, 0) == -1))
        DEATH ("shm_open");

    if (shm_unlink (NAME_SHM))
        DEATH ("shm_unlink");

    printf ("Shared Memory Region successfully destroyed\n");

    if ((mysem = sem_open (NAME_SEM, 0)) == SEM_FAILED)
        DEATH ("sem_open");

    if ((sem_unlink (NAME_SEM)) == -1)
        DEATH ("sem_unlink");

    printf ("Semaphore successfully deleted\n");

    exit (EXIT_SUCCESS);
}

void send_it (void)
{
    int shm_fd, i;
    void *shm_area;
    sem_t *mysem;
```

```
    if ((shm_fd = shm_open (NAME_SHM, O_RDWR, 0)) == -1)
        DEATH ("shm_open");

    shm_area = mmap (NULL, SIZE, PROT_READ | PROT_WRITE, MAP_SHARED, shm_fd, 0);

    if (shm_area == MAP_FAILED)
        DEATH ("mmap");

    printf ("SEND: Memory attached at %lX\n", (unsigned long)shm_area);

    printf ("Attaching to the semaphore\n");

    if ((mysem = sem_open (NAME_SEM, 0)) == SEM_FAILED)
        DEATH ("sem_open");

    for (i = 0; i < 4; i++) {
        if (sem_wait (mysem))
            DEATH ("sem_wait");
        printf ("Please type a message:\n");
        fgets (shm_area, SIZE, stdin);
        if (sem_post (mysem))
            DEATH ("sem_post");
        usleep (1000);          /* pause a millisecond to give other guy a chance */
    }

    if (munmap (shm_area, SIZE))
        DEATH ("munmap");

    if ((sem_close (mysem)) == -1)
        DEATH ("sem_close");

    printf ("SEND has successfully completed\n");

    exit (EXIT_SUCCESS);
}

void receive_it (void)
{
    int shm_fd, i;
    void *shm_area;
    sem_t *mysem;

    if ((shm_fd = shm_open (NAME_SHM, O_RDWR, 0)) == -1)
        DEATH ("shm_open");

    shm_area = mmap (NULL, SIZE, PROT_READ | PROT_WRITE, MAP_SHARED, shm_fd, 0);

    if (shm_area == MAP_FAILED)
        DEATH ("mmap");

    printf ("RCV: Memory attached at %lX\n", (unsigned long)shm_area);

    printf ("Attaching to the semaphore\n");
```

```
    if ((mysem = sem_open (NAME_SEM, 0)) == SEM_FAILED)
        DEATH ("sem_open");

    for (i = 0; i < 4; i++) {
        if (sem_wait (mysem))
            DEATH ("sem_wait");
        fprintf (stdout, "%s\n", (char *)shm_area);
        if (sem_post (mysem))
            DEATH ("sem_post");
        usleep (1000);          /* pause a millisecond to give other guy a chance */
    }

    printf ("RCV has successfully completed\n");

    if (munmap (shm_area, SIZE))
        DEATH ("munmap");

    if ((sem_close (mysem)) == -1)
        DEATH ("sem_close");

    exit (EXIT_SUCCESS);
}

int main (int argc, char *argv[])
{
    if (argc > 1) {
        if (!strcasecmp ("create", argv[1]))
            create_it ();
        if (!strcasecmp ("remove", argv[1]))
            remove_it ();
        if (!strcasecmp ("receive", argv[1]))
            receive_it ();
        if (!strcasecmp ("send", argv[1]))
            send_it ();
    }
    printf ("Usage: %s  create | remove | receive | send \n", argv[0]);
    exit (-1);
}
```

Chapter 32

Message Queues

32.1 Lab 1: Message Queues

- Construct one or more programs that communicate with each other by using message queues. Run them in separate windows.

- The sending program should take lines of input until being given the string "end".

- The receiving program should print out the messages sent.

- You may write more than one program, or write one program that can do multiple actions based on the arguments.

- Two solutions are given; one for System V IPC and one for POSIX IPC.

- The solutions are written so that they take an argument, which can be either `create`, `remove`, `send`, or `receive`, which controls their action.

- Don't forget to compile with `-lrt` for the POSIX IPC solution.

lab1_v_mq.c

```
    /* Copyright 2009, J Cooperstein coop@coopj.com (GPLv2) */
#include <stdlib.h>
#include <stdio.h>
#include <string.h>
#include <unistd.h>
#include <errno.h>

#include <sys/types.h>
#include <sys/ipc.h>
#include <sys/msg.h>

#define BUFSIZE 4096
size_t size = BUFSIZE;

#define DEATH(mess) { perror(mess); exit(errno); }

struct my_msg_st
{
    long my_msg_type;
    char some_text[BUFSIZE];
};

void create_it (void)
{
    int msgid;

    if ((msgid = msgget ((key_t) 1234, 0666 | IPC_CREAT | IPC_EXCL)) == -1)
        DEATH ("msgget");

    printf ("Message Queue successfully created\n");

    exit (EXIT_SUCCESS);
}

void remove_it (void)
{
    int msgid;

    if ((msgid = msgget ((key_t) 1234, 0666)) == -1)
        DEATH ("msgget");

    if (msgctl (msgid, IPC_RMID, 0) == -1)
        DEATH ("msgctl");

    printf ("Message Queue successfully destroyed\n");

    exit (EXIT_SUCCESS);
}

void send_it (void)
{
    int running = 1;
    struct my_msg_st some_data;
    int msgid;
    char buffer[BUFSIZE];
```

```
        if ((msgid = msgget ((key_t) 1234, 0666)) == -1)
            DEATH ("msgget");

        while (running) {
            printf ("Enter some text: ");
            fgets (buffer, BUFSIZE, stdin);
            some_data.my_msg_type = 1;
            strcpy (some_data.some_text, buffer);

            if (msgsnd (msgid, (void *)&some_data, BUFSIZE, 0) == -1)
                DEATH ("msgsnd");

            if (strncasecmp (buffer, "end", 3) == 0) {
                running = 0;
            }
        }

        printf ("SEND has successfully completed\n");

        exit (EXIT_SUCCESS);
}

void receive_it (void)
{
        int running = 1;
        int msgid;
        struct my_msg_st some_data;
        long msg_to_receive = 0;

        if ((msgid = msgget ((key_t) 1234, 0666)) == -1)
            DEATH ("msgget");

        while (running) {
            if (msgrcv (msgid, (void *)&some_data, BUFSIZE,
                        msg_to_receive, 0) == -1)
                DEATH ("msgrcv");

            printf ("You wrote: %s", some_data.some_text);
            if (strncasecmp (some_data.some_text, "end", 3) == 0) {
                running = 0;
            }
        }

        printf ("RECEIVE has successfully completed\n");

        exit (EXIT_SUCCESS);

}

int main (int argc, char *argv[])
{
        if (argc > 1) {
            if (!strcasecmp ("create", argv[1]))
                create_it ();
```

```
        if (!strcasecmp ("remove", argv[1]))
            remove_it ();
        if (!strcasecmp ("receive", argv[1]))
            receive_it ();
        if (!strcasecmp ("send", argv[1]))
            send_it ();
    }
    printf ("Usage: %s  create | remove | receive | send \n", argv[0]);
    exit (-1);
}
```

lab1_p_mq.c

```
 /* Copyright 2009, J Cooperstein coop@coopj.com (GPLv2) */
#include <stdlib.h>
#include <stdio.h>
#include <string.h>
#include <unistd.h>
#include <errno.h>
#include <fcntl.h>
#include <sys/types.h>
#include <mqueue.h>

#define BUFSIZE 4096
#define NAME "/my_mq"

#define DEATH(mess) { perror(mess); exit(errno); }

size_t size = BUFSIZE;
struct mq_attr attr = {
    .mq_maxmsg = 10,
    .mq_msgsize = BUFSIZE,
};

void create_it (void)
{
    mqd_t msg_fd;

    if ((msg_fd = mq_open (NAME, O_RDWR | O_CREAT | O_EXCL, 0666, &attr)) == -1)
        DEATH ("mq_open");

    mq_getattr (msg_fd, &attr);
    printf ("size = %d\n", (int)size);

    if (mq_close (msg_fd))
        DEATH ("mq_close");

    printf ("Message Queue successfully created\n");

    exit (EXIT_SUCCESS);
}

void remove_it (void)
{
    mqd_t msg_fd;
```

```
    if ((msg_fd = mq_open (NAME, O_RDWR, 0, NULL)) == -1)
        DEATH ("mq_open");

    if (mq_close (msg_fd))
        DEATH ("mq_close");

    if (mq_unlink (NAME))
        DEATH ("mq_unlink");

    printf ("Message Queue successfully destroyed\n");

    exit (EXIT_SUCCESS);
}

void send_it (void)
{
    mqd_t msg_fd;
    int running = 1;
    char some_text[BUFSIZE];

    if ((msg_fd = mq_open (NAME, O_RDWR, 0, NULL)) == -1)
        DEATH ("mq_open");

    while (running) {
        printf ("Enter some text: ");
        fgets (some_text, BUFSIZE, stdin);

        if (mq_send (msg_fd, some_text, size, 0) == -1)
            DEATH ("mq_send");

        if (strncasecmp (some_text, "end", 3) == 0)
            running = 0;
    }

    if (mq_close (msg_fd))
        DEATH ("mq_close");

    printf ("SEND has successfully completed\n");

    exit (EXIT_SUCCESS);
}

void receive_it (void)
{
    mqd_t msg_fd;
    int running = 1;
    char some_text[BUFSIZE];

    if ((msg_fd = mq_open (NAME, O_RDWR, 0, NULL)) == -1)
        DEATH ("mq_open");

    printf ("size = %d\n", (int)size);

    while (running) {
```

```
    if (mq_receive (msg_fd, some_text, size, NULL) == -1)
        DEATH ("mq_receive");

    printf ("You wrote: %s", some_text);

    if (strncasecmp (some_text, "end", 3) == 0)
        running = 0;
}

if (mq_close (msg_fd))
    DEATH ("mq_close");

printf ("RECEIVE has successfully completed\n");

exit (EXIT_SUCCESS);

}

int main (int argc, char *argv[])
{
    if (argc > 1) {
        if (!strcasecmp ("create", argv[1]))
            create_it ();
        if (!strcasecmp ("remove", argv[1]))
            remove_it ();
        if (!strcasecmp ("receive", argv[1]))
            receive_it ();
        if (!strcasecmp ("send", argv[1]))
            send_it ();
    }
    printf ("Usage: %s  create | remove | receive | send \n", argv[0]);
    exit (-1);
}
```

14375428R00109

Made in the USA
Charleston, SC
08 September 2012